THE DELTA
IN THE
REARVIEW
MIRROR

THE DELTA
IN THE
REARVIEW
MIRROR

The *Life* and *Death* of *Mississippi's* *First Winery*

Di Rushing

UNIVERSITY PRESS OF MISSISSIPPI / JACKSON

The University Press of Mississippi is the scholarly publishing agency
of the Mississippi Institutions of Higher Learning: Alcorn State University,
Delta State University, Jackson State University, Mississippi State University,
Mississippi University for Women, Mississippi Valley State University,
University of Mississippi, and University of Southern Mississippi.

www.upress.state.ms.us

The University Press of Mississippi is a member
of the Association of University Presses.

Library of Congress Cataloging-in-Publication Data

Names: Rushing, Di, author.
Title: The Delta in the rearview mirror :
the life and death of Mississippi's first winery / Di Rushing.
Description: Jackson : University Press of Mississippi, 2024.
Identifiers: LCCN 2023045371 (print) | LCCN 2023045372 (ebook)
| ISBN 978-1-4968-4929-8 (hardback) | ISBN 978-1-4968-4930-4 (epub)
| ISBN 978-1-4968-4931-1 (epub) | ISBN 978-1-4968-4932-8 (pdf)
| ISBN 978-1-4968-4933-5 (pdf)
Subjects: LCSH: Rushing, Di. | Wineries—Mississippi. | Wine and
wine making—Mississippi. | Delta (Miss. : Region)—Biography
—Anecdotes. | Delta (Miss. : Region)—History, Local—Anecdotes.
Classification: LCC TP557.5.M6 R87 2024 (print) | LCC TP557.5.M6
(ebook) | DDC 663/.2009762—dc23/eng/20231107
LC record available at https://lccn.loc.gov/2023045371
LC ebook record available at https://lccn.loc.gov/2023045372

British Library Cataloging-in-Publication Data available

Dedicated to Sam, Lizzie, and Matt
Thank you for allowing me to tell our story.

CONTENTS

FOREWORD

Sometimes it is difficult for a white woman to write her story set in the Mississippi Delta without coming across as "precious." This is an account I have begun to write every few years, only to set it aside again because it might be too depressing, or too self-aggrandizing, or too self-deprecating. Mostly, I feared that some may perceive it as an indictment of the Delta, where many people I love still live. Whatever the reason, decade after decade, I postponed and proceeded with life. Now, over thirty years later, as I sit in my home in the beautiful mountain town of Ouray, Colorado, waiting out the pandemic, I decide maybe it is time.

I go to the attic and bring down six boxes of decades-old newspaper and magazine clippings. I clear my dining room table and begin the laborious task of sifting through the dozens of articles, one by one. I find fourteen empty cardboard boxes and label them clearly with the dates, 1977 through 1990, one for each year we owned and operated the Winery Rushing near Merigold. Mixed throughout the articles are faded photographs, awards, medals, and letters from customers. I examine each one and place it in the box with the corresponding date. Opening the third box, I find the most recent newspaper article and I set it aside. It is not faded as the others, and its bold headline about a triple murder in Merigold jumps out among the older, yellowed ones.

I brush off a dusty accounts ledger with dog-eared pink invoices sticking out on the top. Affixed to the front cover is a large label: CRIME SEARCH SCENE—EVIDENCE REPORT. I open it and am flooded with memories of calling on wholesale customers from all

over Mississippi—Tupelo, Oxford, Olive Branch, Ocean Springs—
and I can still envision some of the faces of those with whom we
did business so many years ago.

I find a twenty-two-year-old printed email from a prestigious
writer who wanted to explore the rights to our story. He flew in
from Canada and spent a week with us, reading the articles and
interviewing us over countless glasses of wine. He found our journey compelling and wanted to run with it, but my husband and I
eventually nixed the whole idea when we realized how harrowing
it was for us to revisit. He was disappointed, but he understood. In
the bottom of the last sealed carton is a little wooden box contain-
ing five dog collars, carefully wrapped in white tissue.

Our story is an unusual one, a wild ride of joy and loss. It tells of
the unlikely birth of a winery and its companion restaurant in the
heart of the Mississippi Delta and their violent end, fourteen years
later. It is a story of confidence eroded by despair, of security eclipsed
by fear. It is also a story of resilience. I sit at the table with my laptop
and begin to write the only way I know, from the heart, about what
happened many years ago and its effect on me as a human being.

Truth is important to me, so I have given careful consideration
in describing these events as I tell my story. The newspaper and
magazine excerpts are reproduced verbatim, with an occasional use
of ellipses to avoid redundancy. Some of the names in my narrative
have been changed. The dialogue is obviously not precise—these conversations took place over three decades ago—but I have attempted
to recreate the discourse as accurately as possible in spirit, if not in
word. My understanding of the events and what I learned from them
are, of course, subjective. That said, my recounting of them is honest.

For a while, the personal losses we incurred in May of 1990
seemed irreversible. We felt at times that the best of our young lives
might already be behind us. I am happy to say now, that was not
the case. Still, in order to comprehend the enormity of loss we felt
in the months following that spring day, one must first understand
the beautiful wallpaper of our lives before it.

Any Given Day

Summer 1990
Merigold, Mississippi

I wake with a jarring start—No!—and sit straight up, gasping for breath. I throw my legs over the side of the bed and peer out my bedroom window towards the winery, my eyes carefully studying every tree, every suspicious shape silhouetted in the moonlight. Two a.m. and it looks as though everything is still. The winding dirt road parallels the silver rippling thread of the bayou for about two hundred yards, about two football fields, to the north side of the winery, where the ripe grapes are crushed each fall. No blazing fire discernible from here. No old green boat of a car in sight. No dark, surreptitious figures slinking around the parking lot.

I reach down to my nightstand and turn on the soft light. I pick up the dog collars I keep there, twirling them in my palm as I study the little hearts dangling from the loops. A brown one, two blue ones and a rhinestone-studded pink. The engraved names catch the moonlight streaming in from the window. I wonder how they died, all over the course of just a few years. Did he torture them first, or were they quick deaths? How did he get Oreo to come with him? What was Socks thinking when he realized he had made a big mistake? Did the others wonder where we were, why we didn't save them?

I take a deep breath and try to relax the muscles in my shoulders. I unclench the sheets in my fists and sit quietly, trying to calm my heart. The night is peaceful, the crickets are doing their thing, my babies are asleep in the next room and my husband, Sam, is right here, a reassuring form under the light blanket. I lean back to the pillow and study the ceiling, wondering if I will ever be able to sleep again without dreaming of that night. The night someone crept into my little restaurant and left a path of destruction. The night he broke into the winery, opened all the vats, and released thousands of gallons of wine. The night wine slowly trickled from the cellar, down the hill towards the water. The night the Sunflower River ran red.

THE DELTA
IN THE
REARVIEW
MIRROR

CHAPTER 1

Living the Dream

October 10, 1977
Delta Democrat-Times
Greenville, Mississippi
History being made
By James Dickerson

One woman said she thought it was probably a Civil War cemetery for the Confederate dead. Another woman said she thought it looked more like a tomato farm.

Both women are wrong, of course.

What they had seen from a distance was a 35-acre vineyard that belongs to the Winery Rushing, a new family-owned enterprise located three miles east of Merigold. High atop the sloping bluffs that overlook the Sunflower River grow more than 6,000 grape vines, supported by rows of wooden posts and metal braces that glimmer in the sun like thousands of tiny mirrors.

By any standards it's a strange sight in the heartland of the Mississippi Delta.

But no one is in the vineyard right now. Everyone is up on the hill, at the state's first winery, crushing grapes—and the confusion and excitement generated resembles nothing quite so much as it does the ordeal of childbirth.

Sam and I were just twenty-four years old when we opened the doors of the first winery in Mississippi on the bucolic, 350-acre Delta farm that belonged to his grandfather. We didn't feel we were particularly entrepreneurial, or even bold; we just thought a winery would be a sexy, avant-garde venture, challenging for sure, but a lot of fun at the same time. Fun was a high priority for us back then, the underlying justification for almost all the free time and money we spent, being childless and all. We had graduated from Mississippi State University the year before, where Sam had become well acquainted with some of the professors of the new Enology (Winemaking) Department. Those associations, coupled with the love of wine we had developed during our first year of marriage in Europe, planted a seed as we looked around the place and pondered how to make a living on such a relatively small tract of land. Cotton and soybeans, which dominated the vast fields of the Delta back then, required large acreage to be profitable, so they were not viable options for us—that is, unless we were willing to live near the poverty level for the rest of our lives. I told Sam that I was not.

So, each evening after Sam spent his day testing soil for local farmers and I returned home from working at nearby Delta State College, we sat on the swing of our run-down front porch, swaying back and forth in an old wicker loveseat hanging from squeaky chains, drinking wine, listening to the Rolling Stones, and speculating about our future. We discussed everything from raising ostriches to keeping bees, but our dream of starting the first winery in Mississippi since Prohibition continuously overshadowed the others. The seed grew as swiftly as the strong current of the Sunflower River, winding its way towards the Yazoo, just down the hill from our porch. The main obstacle, of course, was money. When I told Sam one evening that I could probably handle being poor for a couple of years while we got on our feet, he ran with it.

I wish I could report that we created sophisticated business plans and spread sheets and consulted countless enologists and accountants, but that would be inaccurate; the truth is, we didn't know what the hell we were doing most of the time. Luckily, the folks at the local bank were almost as excited about the proposal as we were. The handwriting was already on the wall about Delta agriculture, and they knew that small farmers were going to have to get creative if they wanted to survive the giant surge of corporations swallowing up the rich land around us. In retrospect, I don't think we knew what a long shot it was, growing a winery in the middle of a lonely cotton field, until we were long gone from the place, decades later. But grow it we did, creating a joyful life in the process.

Sam spent the winter days of 1977 digging postholes, attaching steel braces, and stringing wire for the vines to embrace, planting just over thirty acres of grapes in all. Nights were spent drifting aimlessly in a sea of cryptic legalese, as we completed paperwork for the State of Mississippi and the US Bureau of Alcohol, Tobacco and Firearms. When the application was finally approved for Mississippi Native Winery Number One, we celebrated large with friends, family, and fireworks over the Sunflower.

The following spring, Sam lovingly planted over six thousand muscadine vines at the feet of wooden posts, talking to them softly as he navigated the rows. He found a wonderful helpmate in Jack, a young man from Merigold who would be with us for our entire journey of fourteen years. Together they plowed, planted, and prayed that the vines would take root in their new home in the rich Delta soil. That they did; we lost fewer than ten grapevines the following season.

During those first couple of years, I continued working in the financial aid office at Delta State. It was fine, but it was not where my heart was. Every day at 5:00, I would rush home, change clothes, and get to work on the old dairy barn that would soon become the tasting and bottling rooms at the Winery Rushing. It was my goal to create a space that was reminiscent of the centuries-old wineries we had frequented in Germany and France, with rustic wooden beams and stucco. With the help of Sam's grandfather, I covered every inch of the exterior with plaster, then painted it a gleaming white. We rescued antique cypress crossties from the shed out back and attached them to the side of the building, creating an old-world look. We constructed brick pathways and bordered them with cypress trees and bright flowers. We washed windows until they sparkled and painted the old cement floor a lovely grass green. Once the first phase of the vineyard was completed, Sam began excavating the eastern slope of the building that led to the river below to build a cellar which would eventually house huge stainless steel wine tanks and small oak barrels.

As exciting as that first year was, the real reward came in the following days as more and more people grew to love and support our venture. People from all walks of life strolled through our doors and enriched our lives in meaningful ways. Sometimes they bought wine and sometimes they brought wine, terrible concoctions they had fermented in their back-room closets, out of the sight of the preacher should he happen by. We always praised it, of course. And they always complimented ours in return. I like to think their accolades were a bit more justified, but Sam and I were both a little intoxicated ourselves by the novelty of it all that first year or two, so I guess we'll never know.

Six years after we opened the winery, we decided that a small restaurant might be a good way to showcase the winery. By that time, we had a two-year old daughter, so my time was a bit more limited, but the idea grew legs quickly. A few months later, Top of the Cellar Tea Room opened its doors for the first time, serving lunch only, five days a week. Overnight it seemed I had made hundreds of new friends, many of whom came every week to eat at the small, renovated tenant shack. A few years after we opened the tea room, an English professor from Ole Miss told me that my place had earned the reputation of "where the elite meet to eat," but I didn't think that was true, nor did I want it to be. To most folks, it was just a quiet, lovely place in the Delta where one could drink some local wine, have a leisurely lunch, and enjoy the beautiful countryside—sort of an Italian Agriturismo, without the overnight stay, of course. It was, by all accounts, unique in place and time.

We have all had epiphanies in life from time to time, some life-changing, others, not so much. Often, we don't recognize their significance for a while. But there was one instance, one blinding lightning bolt, that I recall as clearly as though it occurred just moments ago. It was a dark winter day just before Christmas 1986. I was working at the tea room, clearing the table in the private dining room. The small gas heater sat in the corner, working hard to counter the freezing rain outside, and the aroma of warm wassail drifted throughout the small rooms of the restaurant. Dried muscadine vines woven through fresh holly and white narcissus provided the centerpiece of the pine farm table. I can still envision the party sitting there, eight beautifully dressed women from nearby Cleveland, all chatting away about something or other. Suddenly, I realized that I was unabashedly, insanely happy. Like everyone, we had our share of problems of course, but I was rocked with joy as I stood there watching some of my favorite customers merrily exchange small Christmas gifts as they sipped their wine. I knew our children were thriving, our business was growing, and our health was good, and I was profoundly grateful. Like most highs in life, that moment of euphoria was unsustainable, of course. But the memory of it helps me appreciate the transitory nature of raw emotion—joy, and more importantly its flip side, fear.

Three years and some change later, Thursday, May 3, 1990, found our young family of four still living in what's known in the Mississippi Delta as "high cotton." We were in our fourteenth year in the wine business, had won eight national awards, and were enjoying brisk sales. Our lovely winery sat on one of the most beautiful spots in the Delta, and Top of the Cellar Tea Room was booked solid for lunch most days. Over eight thousand gallons of wine were aging in the cellar, and we were on the verge of expanding nationwide. A permanent showroom at the Dallas World Trade Mart showcased our growing line of gourmet mixes. We had been successful in securing federal recognition of the Delta as an official viticultural area, the second largest in the United States, and had just designed a new wine label featuring the great blues players of the Delta. Our vineyard across the bayou was budding nicely, and Jack and the crew were pumped for the new crop. Shiny equipment had been purchased from Europe and plans for expansion of the winery and tea room were on the table. Our dreams for the future looked very bright.

But life comes at you fast sometimes.

By the next day, Friday, May 4, all those dreams had shattered.

CHAPTER 2

An Otherwise Lovely Spring Morning

Preface from *House Specialties of Top of the Cellar Tea Room*
By Diane Paul Rushing

Seventeen years and two children later find Sam and me still hur-
dling some hitches, but I know few people who enjoy life as we
do. Granted, it's no Falcon Crest life that we lead at the Winery
Rushing, but we do find ourselves surrounded daily by customers
we love and many of whom love us back.

The morning it started was already hectic. I was in the kitchen putting the finishing touches on the hundred or so strawberry short-
cakes my daughter and I had prepared the night before for May Day
Play Day, the highlight of the year at her school, with athletic games,
music, and a fine picnic. Music from Fraggle Rock blared from the
TV in the living room, where my five-year-old son sat cross-legged
on the floor eating Cheerios floating in milk.

"Matt! Turn that off and get ready for school!" I called from the
kitchen. The volume dropped immediately, but that was the only
acknowledgment that I had been heard. Sassy, our new black lab
puppy, squatted at that exact moment and looked me straight in the
eye as she wet the kitchen floor. I detected no evidence of shame on

her shiny little face. "Of course you just did that," I muttered, placing another dessert into the box on the counter.

Lizzie suddenly appeared at the doorway to the kitchen and said that she was wearing her Cinderella dress to school. I thought how, of all the days in the school year, this was the worst she could have chosen to go all formal on me. The day's agenda, with its sack races, Red Rover, and other archaic games, called for old jeans and faded T-shirts. I took a deep breath and looked at my eight-year-old in her sparkly blue dress and sapphire-studded tiara. She struck a self-righteous pose and waited for my reaction. We studied each other for a long moment as we engaged in the familiar contest of wills.

Nope, I decided. *I'm not doin' this today.*

"Sure," I told her. "Why not?" She squealed and dashed off to put on her shoes.

My first hint that something was wrong was when I picked up the phone to call the school to find out where to drop off the desserts. Our home phone was an extension of the winery's, and after a second of frustration in hearing voices, I listened for the conversation to end. A deep voice I didn't recognize was asking my husband to confirm something about . . . the wine? Then I heard Sam reply frantically, "Yes! It's ankle deep in the cellar, and it's all going down the drain! Please, y'all get here as fast as you can!"

The man replied, "Yessir. We'll be right there."

"Sam!" I said, "What the hell is going on down there?" Click. Crickets. He had hung up.

I ran the box of desserts out to the car and quickly finished getting the kids ready for school. I called Mary Beth, a neighbor with whom we had carpooled for several years and asked if she could pick them up at the winery. Grabbing their backpacks, I stuffed them into the back seat of the car alongside Lizzie and Matt. They were confused by the sudden turn of events, especially when I told them not to worry about their seat belts—we're just going to the winery. Both were uncharacteristically quiet as I stormed from the driveway in a cloud of dust.

Thirty seconds later, a terrified child on each side, I stood frozen in the parking lot, the strong essence of wine drifting through the open door. The kids knew that something terrible had happened, and their imaginations were darting around their little heads like pinballs. "Where's Daddy?" they repeated over and over, their small voices quivering, despite my reassuring that he was fine, just busy. Suddenly I realized how critical it was that they see for themselves, so the three of us went inside.

Holding hands, we walked through the tasting room and toward the door to the wine cellar, following ominous tracks of large red drops on the pale green floor. In my muddled state of mind, I thought I was looking at a trail of blood, and I stopped cold. Bending over slowly, I ran my index finger through one of the drops and was flooded with relief as I saw that it was red wine. I gripped my children's hands once again and continued through the gift area, shelves laden with neatly stacked T-shirts sporting our proud brand: The Winery Rushing. Wine glasses printed with the tea room logo sparkled in the display lights from overhead. Dozens of bottles of Rushing Wine nestled in wooden wine racks that lined the north side of the tasting room. A few had been yanked out and lay broken on the floor, crimson contents trickling towards the drain in the adjacent bottling room. Above the wood stove, the ceiling fan revolved slowly, crooning its customary hum. As we walked past an antique sideboard displaying corkscrews for sale, its beveled mirror caught my reflection, startling me so that both children looked up at me in panicked fear. I told myself to get a grip and continued toward the door leading to the cellar.

The three of us paused at the top of the stairs. The old wooden steps, stained by a decade of wine spills, seemed at once sinister and inviting. The aroma of red wine was overpowering, suffocating. Standing there, we could hear Sam's muttering from below as he surveyed the huge, now empty, stainless-steel tanks. His expletives, despondent and incoherent, seemed directed at no one, but their aching frustration echoed to where we stood above.

"Sam?" I called into the stairwell. "Are you okay?" My voice reverberated in the vast space below. No response.

"Daddy?" Lizzie whimpered.

Bad move on my part, I thought, *bringing the kids here*, but this concern was quickly alleviated by the relief on their faces when Sam began to climb the steps from the cellar. His shoes and pant legs were soaked in red wine, and his right hand gripped a shattered piece of oak from one of the barrels below. The look on his handsome face was one I had never seen in the seventeen years we had been married, a stark reflection of simultaneous grief, anger, and bewilderment. The kids ran to him as he bent down, pulling them close, looking up at me with countless questions in his eyes. "Gone . . . it's all gone," he said. Lizzie and Matt clung to him, crying, unable to process this devastating destruction and its pernicious sidekick, helplessness.

I think at that moment, as Sam and I held our children in a huddle at the top of the stairs, all four of us knew on varying levels that our lives were forever changed, that the mostly charmed existence we had enjoyed before this moment would be altered in some inconceivable way. We loved our routine—the comfortable, mundane cycle of work, play, and school—and I felt certain that this lifestyle was somehow coming to an end. In retrospect, I see that it was at this precise moment that I internalized the truth that any control we may think we have is an illusion, a trick played on our minds to keep us reasonably sane as we navigate life. The realization was paralyzing.

Gazing into the stairwell leading to the cellar, I suddenly jerked back up to attention. "Sam! Have you been to the tea room?"

He studied me for a moment and then nodded. "Yeah, I have. It's pretty much . . . well," he said, fumbling for words.

Saying nothing more, he bent down and gathered Matt up into his arms. Lizzie and I followed them past the water fountain near the bar with its playful sign, "Pinot de Pump," now defaced by a hard kick delivered the night before. We continued through the office and into the lab, where we saw a broken window and glass scattered beneath it. The only other anomaly was an overturned beaker of red wine on the counter. As we left the winery and followed the old brick sidewalk to the front door of the tea room, we heard water trickling, along with the normal morning sounds of air conditioners running and birds tweeting.

We stepped onto the front porch. The placard by the front door, "Welcome to Top of the Cellar Tea Room," was broken in two and thrown onto a wicker chair by the entrance. The blue French door was demolished, sharp shards of glass protruding from each frame. The sound of running water grew louder, and the ominous odor of propane wafted from inside. I peered through a broken pane in the door. Tables were overturned and chairs sat at obscene angles among them. Blue and white sugar bowls and saltshakers lay in fragments, scattered on the floor. The hand-carved easel holding a chalk board featuring the previous day's menu stood absurdly intact, witness to the night's devastation. The doors leading to the screened porch overlooking the Sunflower River were half off their hinges, and the cash box lay nearby on its side, open and empty, save for a few coins.

A thin thread of water made its way from the hallway that led to the restroom, puddling in the middle of the dining room. Blue linen napkins and place mats from tables set the afternoon before soaked in the shallow pool. A white place card from a reserved table was sitting erect on the floor, positioned just inside the door. Campbell. From Tallahatchie County. One of my most beloved patrons. Its presence there seemed obscene. I'll have to call them. I'll have to cancel everyone's reservations, won't I?

Taking my children's hands once again, I stepped away from the porch and led them back toward the parking lot in front of the winery. We sat silently on the bench, waiting for Mary Beth to pick them up for school. We looked across the bayou and observed dust billowing in the wake of Jack's red tractor as he drove a turn row in the vineyard. We listened as a crop duster flew low overhead, headed toward our neighbor's farm to the west. Lizzie inched closer to me, smoothing out the wrinkles in her Cinderella dress, a solemn look on her face. I held Matt's small hand in mine as he counted the few cars that sped past on the road.

I was grateful that my children were well on their way to school by the time the sheriff's car pulled up in front of the winery, red and blue lights flashing under an impossibly blue Delta sky.

CHAPTER 3

A Nice Place to Visit

December 27, 1985
Oxford Times
Oxford, Mississippi
Restaurant Review: Top of the Cellar
By Mike Wall and Don Stanford

. . . The three hungry members in our crowd were seated in a cozy little room with a glowing gas heater nearby and were immediately served an ice-cold glass of sweet, fruity muscadine wine. Within ten minutes, we were treated to a steaming crock of broccoli soup, a generous slice of ham and spinach quiche, a square of cranberry salad, and homemade wine muffins. The broccoli soup was thick but smooth and warm and had big, juicy chunks of spicy broccoli, celery and onions that warmed our throats on the way down. The quiche was golden brown and had an almost perfect consistency, not too crumbly but not too soft, with morsels of baked ham and chopped spinach and a hearty flavor. The steaming muffins, soon smothered with soft yellow butter, were a delightful accompaniment to the soup and quiche.

. . . Enchanted with the aroma of after-dinner coffee and satisfied with full tummies, we were able to chat with Diane about the restaurant. Normally, she offers a choice of two entrees. The one we were not able to sample today was poppyseed chicken with french cut green beans. Meals also include complimentary wine and appetizers.

The most striking aspect of the entire visit was the fact that Diane treated us so warmly though we had not complied with her policy of reservations, and she had just served several large groups. She told us that the only reason she asks for reservations is that the winery is located several miles from the closest store, and it is sometimes difficult to anticipate how much to prepare if she is swamped by unexpected guests.

"So, who's mad at you?" The sheriff surveyed the tea room and the considerable damage that had been left behind. "This seems," he said, pausing for the right word, "personal." Each rectangle of glass in every window and door had been tapped out, as though someone had leisurely strolled along the wall with a ball-peen hammer, making several passes back and forth to ensure that each antique, wavy pane was destroyed. No one had been in a big hurry here; that was for sure. Even the toilet in the cypress-paneled bathroom had been smashed, the largest piece no larger than a teacup. And water was everywhere. Fortunately, the art on the walls had been spared, overlooked no doubt, but this small piece of luck was important to me because they framed pieces of intricate embroidery hand-stitched by my grandmother and her mother a century before.

The smell of gas was overpowering as we stepped toward the kitchen. The stove was pulled out from the wall, exposing the gas valve attached to the pipe behind it, and the oven door was open. As Sam bent down to shut off the gas line, the sheriff spoke again.

"Turn that knob tight now, Sam," he said. "I'll open the door and get some fresh air in here." He stepped past me and opened the back door leading to the winery.

"Why would they turn the gas on?" I wondered, as I looked around the kitchen. A white porcelain cream pitcher sat pristine on the shelf over the sink, just inches away from a matching sugar bowl, crushed into a pile of tiny fragments.

"Oh, I expect I know, all right," said the sheriff as he helped Sam push the stove back into place. "He was trying to blow the place up."

"What?" I must have misunderstood.

The sheriff rubbed his face and looked at me. "Whoever did all this was trying to blow the whole place up," he repeated. "But by breakin' all the windows out, he pretty much undermined his own efforts. Dumb son of a . . . sorry, Di." He was obviously shaken, crossing his arms and shaking his head slowly.

The winery and tea room were a source of pride in the Delta, a place where people brought visitors from out of town, a place where they met their friends for a fun outing to the country. This was the kitchen where Roberta, Flo, Shirley, and I met each weekday morning at nine o'clock to turn on some music, mix up some wine muffins, set some tables, and cook whatever was the plat du jour. Over the years we had fine-tuned these daily tasks, making them quite manageable, even on the days we served over fifty guests from all over the South. Open for lunch only, Top of the Cellar Tea Room was tailored to fit our schedules. Roberta enjoyed her Saturdays and Sundays off, Shirley was a night student at Delta State, and Flo and I both had school-aged children. Typically, there were two seatings, one at 11:30 and another at 1:00, although we were flexible when we could be. Reservations were not required but certainly recommended. We had our regulars with standing reservations from the environs of course, but also quite a few from Memphis, which lay one hundred miles to the north, and Jackson, two hours and some change south. The tea room was quite simple in its day-to-day operation, out of necessity, I might add. My degree was in English, not culinary arts, and part of me was always waiting for some tall dude in a long black trench coat to burst through the door of the place.

"There she is! There's that girl who is pretending to be a cook!" Then I would slither away at the shame of being caught. Mine was a classic case of imposter syndrome in those early years at the tea room.

Each day we offered a choice of two plates at Top of the Cellar. In the summers, our clientele knew that if they didn't want the daily special, they could rely on ordering the summer plate, which was the same each day, each summer, for seven years. This featured a wonderful toasted almond chicken salad, cold marinated green beans, a fruit concoction of some sort, and a wine muffin. Our winter plate, the daily alternative in colder months, was a generous slice of homemade quiche, a bowl of rich mushroom soup, warm curried fruit and again, the ubiquitous wine muffin. My wine muffins were a hit, and within a year I was selling the mix and generating almost as much income as the restaurant did. That same year I started marketing our mulling spice, which we served warm at the tea room during the winter months. Rebranded as Rocky Mountain Wassail Spice Blend after we moved to Colorado, today it is the sole survivor of those days and is still sold in most states.

As an alternative to the summer and winter plates, we offered another menu that changed every day and repeated every three weeks or so. Of course, some were more popular than others, but we got varying degrees of accolades on them all. We also offered a choice of two desserts and what I would describe as mediocre coffee or tea. All of this, and a 15 percent tip, could get a person in and out for around $10. We soon became friends with our patrons, and the repartee punctuated by boisterous laughter in the tea room resounded every day when we opened those doors. Black ladies and white ladies flowed through the door dressed to a T, ready for their complimentary samples of wine and parmesan cheese biscuits.

The main dining room walls were covered with a soft yellow wallpaper featuring Asian red blossoms and blue and green birds perched on brown branches. The vaulted ceiling and trim were cut from pecky cypress from our farm and stained a rich Dutch blue. The old light fixture had supposedly come from the main train depot in Memphis torn down many years earlier, but I was never sure about that; the antique dealer from whom I bought it seemed somewhat dubious in describing its provenance. The French doors off the main dining room led to a screened-in porch overlooking a stunning view, the green pasture dotted with cypress trees leading down the hill to the edge of the Sunflower River.

From that viewpoint, over the years, our family had watched more than one baptism conducted by a nearby African Methodist Episcopal (A.M.E.) Church preacher. Each spring, Black people of all ages dressed in glorious white robes and gathered just below the bridge on our farm, as they had been doing for decades, to ceremoniously "wash away their sins." This picturesque scene would have been indistinguishable from one a hundred years earlier, were it not for the dozen or so cars and trucks parked along the road just west of the bridge. The tall, slender Reverend stood waist deep in the river, extending his hand as, one by one, men, women and children carefully made their way down to the muddy bank for the annual ritual. His benevolent smile and calm reassurances were discernible even from where we watched, thirty yards up the hill. The white gowns billowed in the cool, silky water as the Reverend gently placed his right hand behind their heads and instructed them to cross both arms over his left arm above their chests. Holding firmly, he gently lowered them into the river until they were completely immersed.

"I baptize you in the name of the Father, the Son, and the Holy Ghost," he chanted, his powerful voice resounding over the crowd. As he lifted the drenched congregant from the water, a jubilant "Hallelujah, Praise God!" boomed throughout the crowd. When the last baptism was completed, the singing began, and the melodious a cappella spirituals continued for an hour or more. Watching the service unfold, my family always felt as though we were unworthy outsiders, surreptitiously witnessing something very special.

Eighty years earlier, another church, White Cloud Baptist, had stood just where our house was situated on the farm. Decades before we arrived, in the name of that dream-crusher called Progress, it had been razed by the previous owners, the beloved tombstones irreverently plowed down the hill into the bayou. One could still see some of the rudimentary stone markers when the water was low, partially hidden by fecund foliage. It was an ignominious end to a glorious gathering place, and I was heartsick about its disrespectful demise.

Also overlooking the Sunflower River was the private dining room, paneled with cypress planks three feet wide, a testament to their age before our part of the Delta was cleared for agriculture in the early 1900s. This cozy room was decorated in soft peach, and the table was always set with fresh flowers. A large urn of willow branches sat in the corner, and Sam's pen-and-ink drawings of the vineyard graced the walls. The quiet seclusion of this highly coveted table was appealing to bankers and planters and clientele who had some really good (private) stories to pass along. We liked to tell our patrons that this room easily seated ten friends or four in-laws. Through the window of this room, one could see the brick pathway that led from the winery to the tea room, bordered by colorful flowerbeds overstuffed with zinnias, periwinkle and, of course, marigolds.

The typical visit to our place called for lunch at Top of the Cellar followed by a visit to the winery next door. There they would be entertained Delta style with a guided tour of the winery followed by wine tasting at the bar, inevitably cheerful and sprinkled with a lot of laughter. Some folks extended the tour by driving across the little bridge in front of our house over to the vineyard, which was a sight to behold, especially in the fall. It was not uncommon for vineyard manager Jack to stop his tractor and answer any questions the guests may have, a crucial part of his job in fact.

Jack worked for us from the day we opened in 1977 until the day we closed in 1990. He and Sam worked side by side, first building a trellis system over the thirty-acre parcel of our 350-acre farm, then planting the muscadines and keeping them properly pruned. When working together, they laughed all day about one thing or another. As the muscadines grew up the trellises, so did our relationship with Jack grow into something strong and timeless. He drove our small red Massey-Ferguson tractor everywhere he went on the farm. Little was more satisfying to me in those days than stopping for a chat with Jack on a hot Delta summer afternoon with Lizzie and Matt in tow. He always started by asking how we were doing and finished with an update on the progress of the vineyard, even though it was hardly part of my wheelhouse. He also loved talking about his wife and kids, proud of the lives they had built in Merigold.

Hailing from farms and rural communities, many of our visitors were more interested in the happenings on this side of the bayou than at the winery and tea room. They were fascinated by the yields of the muscadine crops and how little acreage it took to supply the needs of the winery. These were the days when cotton was slowly being deposed as "King," and other crops such as rice and soybeans were being grown on a large scale for the first time in the Delta's relatively short agricultural history. In the fall, driving the turn rows between the silver trellises sagging with ripe muscadines was an incredibly pleasant experience in sensory overload. The sweet odor of ripe grapes perfectly complemented the burgundy fruit and green foliage. Jack loved this spot on the planet as much as we did it seemed, and he became quite the viticulturist during his years with us. He especially enjoyed passing time with farmers who were as interested as he was in the operations at the vineyard.

"How're y'all doin' today?" Jack greeted them, stepping down from the little tractor and dusting himself off with his ball cap as he walked toward their vehicle. On hot days, these folks, mostly retired, just rolled down the windows and sat in comfort as they conversed, frigid air barreling from their air-conditioned cars. Jack would smile as he leaned down to talk to them, hands propped on his knees. And as all of them learned, he was a great listener. Their eyes and smiles lit up as they shared memories of picking and eating wild muscadines hanging from giant cypress trees in the bayou. They talked about carrying gunnysacks up thousand-year-old trees, those huge living dinosaurs of the Delta growing straight out of the waters of the bayous. They described dodging water moccasins and swatting mosquitoes big enough to carry them away as they plucked the fruit from the vines. They especially loved telling Jack about the homemade wine they made after these hazardous excursions into the canebrakes, bragging about how strong it was, as if that were the true sign of enological excellence.

"Y'all never did smoke those vines now, did ya?" Jack often teased, a toothpick hanging from his mouth. One would think he had never heard of such outrageous behavior as he laughed at their denial, or even better, their admission to this common, "sinful" practice. He never seemed to tire of the repetition, which made everyone love him even more.

Almost all our visitors left the winery with good memories, a few bottles of wine, and a plan to return soon. And for most of them, the next stop was three miles west, to the famous McCarty's Pottery in Merigold. Those who knew the ropes knew that the timing for a visit there was perfect, for it was about then that Lee McCarty was rising from his daily nap and sitting down at his pottery wheel, ready to regale the world once again with his outrageously funny anecdotes of life in the Mississippi Delta.

CHAPTER 4

Mississippi Mud

January 1, 1989
Greenwood Commonwealth
Greenwood, Mississippi
Art in Mississippi: Merigold
By Susan Montgomery

The McCartys are known nationally—and even internationally—for their work and for the way they live. Their property is surrounded by tall wooden fences and bamboo, which encase gardens and rooms full of artwork, including shelves and shelves of their pottery. Plates and cups, vases, trays and bowls. And figures of animals. Squirrels, lambs, rabbits, frogs, birds. Among these things is Lee McCarty, wearing khaki slacks, two cotton shirts—one white, one blue—and eyeglasses slipping down his nose.

"We just got back from walking around with the people of Japan—as their guests," he said. The government had brought them to Japan because of their art, which includes not only pottery but Pup McCarty's enameling. They came home with the inspiration for a new piece. "We realized," said McCarty, "that we could make those gorgeous lanterns." He pointed to an unfinished lantern, wrought from clay rather than paper.

"Ain't that McCarty's pottery?" the sheriff asked as he assessed the damage to my broken kitchen. The cheerful sound of birds singing on the other side of the screened door seemed oddly incongruous to the destruction surrounding us.

"Yes, Sir," I replied. "That's all we use here." I surveyed the cinnamon-colored bowls and plates on the shelves over the counter, grateful that they had been spared. Seven years earlier, upon learning that we were opening the tea room, Lee and Pup McCarty had called and insisted on donating "anything y'all want for the place." The flat brown stoneware added a nice touch to our food presentation and served as a reminder to guests of how special our little corner of the Delta was. Each plate, bowl, and cup was branded with the distinguished McCarty mark, an inch-long crooked streak winding its way to the edge of the piece, symbolic of the Mississippi River.

The McCartys had been supportive of Sam's and my crazy endeavors since we started in 1977, and they continued to be for many years to come. Six months after our young family relocated to Colorado in 1990, I opened the door of our new shop in downtown Ouray one morning to find the UPS driver unloading box after box from his truck onto the sidewalk.

"Excuse me, Sir, but I think you must have the wrong address," I said, trying to save him a little work. "We haven't ordered anything."

"Is this Ouray Glassworks?" he asked. "325 Sixth Avenue?"

"Well, yes, but I can't imagine what all this could be."

"Says here it's from McCarty Pottery, in ummm . . . Merigold, Mississippi. And it's addressed to Ouray Glassworks." He paused and looked up at me, his hands on a box on the sidewalk. "That you?"

Confused but curious, I nodded and told him to go ahead and unload it, about twenty large, heavy boxes in all. As soon as he pulled away, I hurried to tell Sam, who was on the side of the building blowing glass in front of an audience of ten or so people. Excited, I told him about the mysterious boxes sitting in the middle of our shop.

Sam shrugged and said, "Call McCarty," so I did. But first, I opened some of the boxes, intrigued by what had been lovingly packed and shipped from over a thousand miles away.

The first few boxes contained rabbits, dozens of beautiful brown clay ones, large and small. As I carefully unpacked the bundles, I recognized the shapes of a few, including my favorites, Mo and Flo, short for Beatrix Potter's Mopsey and Flopsey. Most had no names, but they were splendid in their identities, nonetheless. Other boxes held wonderfully crafted cats, one named T. S. Eliot in honor of his playful take on feline philosophy. I forget now all the distinguished honorifics the McCartys had appointed their tasteful little critters, but most reflected a distinct appreciation for fine literature. I unwrapped box after box of beautiful little woodland creatures, as well as candle plates, wind chimes, angels, bowls, cups, and platters. I calculated there was around eight thousand dollars' worth of pottery sitting in the wrinkled newspaper strewn about the floor of our small shop. Why, I had no idea.

I picked up the phone and called McCarty, whose number I had long before memorized. He answered the phone with his slow, beautifully accented, "McCarty's."

"Lee, this is Di. We just got a huge shipment of pottery from your place. It's great and everything, but . . . what the hell?"

"Well, Di," he began. I could hear the smile in his voice. "Pup and I knew y'all are trying to get going again and we knew Sam was just starting to blow glass and we just figured y'all just needed something to sell until he got his inventory up and everything."

"Well, that is certainly true, Lee, but we can't possibly pay for all of this." Never had truer words been spoken. Those were the days we sometimes found ourselves searching the couch cushions for quarters to go to Apteka Drug Store and buy a Coke.

"Y'all don't have to pay us, now or ever," he replied. He then went on to explain something to the effect that they had a whole lot of money, and we didn't have any. And that was also a fact.

McCarty's in Merigold was world renowned by then, not only for its pottery but for the beautiful milieu they had created to display and sell their wares. Set in a dense cane break in the middle of town, with twenty-foot-tall cypress fencing enclosing the entire cool, quiet oasis, McCarty's was the kind of place that is impossible to define. A few original Georgia O'Keefe paintings graced the walls, the faint smell of lavender combined with earthy clay permeated the many small spaces, and the gentle sounds of McCarty wind chimes resonated throughout. Famous people from around the world graced these elegant quarters from time to time. The diminutive and gracious Pup gently floated about the premises in her signature white linen, projecting elegance and simplicity. Husband Lee was her perfect foil—disheveled and covered in Mississippi mud clay, sitting at his potter's wheel. He was the very definition of the Southern Man.

It was Lee who told me when I was in my early twenties that an important distinction between Southerners and Northerners was that in the South, we are more appreciative of our eccentric friends and relatives because they add much color to our lives. We had been discussing Tom, an old citizen of Merigold who had recently been found with six years' worth of uncashed Social Security checks in his pockets. In total, they came to about $36,000. The temperature in the Delta that day was a humid 95 degrees, and he was wearing a wool coat with a padlock over the front opening. He had fallen while scrounging through the trash behind the gas station, and the town had rallied with strong support throughout his recovery.

"We don't squirrel away our quirky old folks like they do up North," Lee posited, holding a bowl as his potter's wheel turned steadily. Turning beautiful pottery was as natural to Lee as breathing, and I marveled at the ease he exhibited as he worked. "We cherish them here," he continued. "We put them on the front porch and show 'em off."

Not sure that I agreed, I shook my head and laughed. "C'mon, Lee. You know that's not always the case. Just look at some of Faulkner's characters. Look at *The Sound and the Fury*, for starters."

"Exactly!" Lee said. "Faulkner absolutely adored the Compsons of the world. That's why he wrote about them so poignantly," he said. I pondered what he said and admitted to myself that he might have a point.

"You do know, Di," he concluded a moment later, looking at me over the top of his glasses. I wondered how he could see anything through the mud smeared on the lens. "Pup and I knew William Faulkner quite well. We became good friends after we moved to Oxford after the war." He then went on to describe how the great writer had allowed young Lee and Pup to dig up some clay from a ravine behind Rowan Oak, the beautiful estate in the hills of Mississippi where Faulkner had retired. He said that from that clay came some of their first pieces of pottery. Lee's unique take on life made a lot more sense once I had learned about this association from his past.

One summer afternoon in the midseventies, Sam and I were strolling with Lee and Pup through "the barn," as they called their gallery/compound. We had stepped outside into the bamboo brakes to cool off and have a chat. We looked around at the fabulous fountains and the hand-carved benches and the gently blowing towers of cane. A lovely blue pool was shimmering in the sunlight, and mourning doves were cooing. The breeze was uncharacteristically cool and crisp. Pup lifted her face into the fresh air, closed her eyes, and took a deep breath. The four of us sat in wicker chairs that graced the poolside, McCarty wind chimes tinkling gently in the wind. Lee took a sip of his iced tea and a slow smile spread across his weathered face.

"Isn't it glorious?" he said in his beautifully cadenced voice, surveying the tranquil environment he and Pup had created together, a harmonious convergence of nature and art. I looked around appreciatively and likewise savored the ambience. I reckoned he was preparing to wax poetic about the spectacular weather we were having or some other lofty notion, but that wasn't the case.

"Isn't it just glorious," Lee repeated, "what a whole lot of money can do?"

CHAPTER 5

What Passes for Inspection

August 28, 1985
Bolivar Commercial
Cleveland, Mississippi
Top of the Cellar Down-home quality draws tea room guests
By Tim McWilliams

. . . Keeping the tea room going requires a team effort. Mrs. Rushing keeps it that way with a little help from her friends in the kitchen. "This is very much a team effort," she said. "Nobody out here has a title and no one is the boss. We're all floor sweepers when the floors need to be swept," she said. "The dining room opens at 11:30 and I leave the kitchen to work out front." . . .

"I was worried about location, but it has turned out to be our biggest drawing card. There's just no place in Mississippi where you can come sample a wine that was made 20 feet away from grapes grown half a mile away." . . . It's a journey the Rushings measure by the heart.

"Folks around here sure loved this place," the sheriff remarked as he walked through the tattered remains of the main dining room and towards the small private dining room. "Been here a few times myself."

Aware of his use of the past tense, I bit my lip and looked around at this old sharecropper's house that we had lovingly renovated from top to bottom. We had moved the house from a farm not too far away, which is a fairly common practice in the Delta. After that, we had spent weeks cleaning, polishing, wallpapering, and painting, restoring its modest charm.

The tea room was a wonderful place to eat, play and work, primarily because of the people who showed up to help me every day. Roberta was the main cook. She would have been labeled a "gourmet chef" in a different place and time, but had I called her that, she would have burst into laughter at my pretentiousness. Roberta was a strong, beautiful woman in her fifties who worked for me from the first happy day we opened the tea room in the summer of 1983 until the sad, defeated day we closed in the final days of 1990. Her voice was musical in its inflection, precise in its diction. She was also resourceful, and I doubt I could have made a go of the place without her wisdom and direction, not to mention her incredible cooking.

Roberta lived in an historic all-Black community two miles north of Merigold, which was three miles west of the winery. Mound Bayou has a rich history, founded in the late nineteenth century by former slaves. Its founder, Isaiah Montgomery, was close friends with Booker T. Washington, who provided much guidance for the genesis of this innovative community. From the late nineteenth century until the early twentieth, it was billed as a land of promise for Black people seeking autonomy, and it continued to thrive until the Great Migration of the 1930s.

Roberta was a native daughter of Mound Bayou and proud of her heritage. Her father's brother was the famous boxer Sonny Liston, world heavyweight champion until his surprise defeat in 1964 by the young upstart Cassius Clay, who later changed his name to Muhammad Ali. But it would be misleading for me to say that Roberta wore this association as a badge of honor; indeed, I had known her for more than a year before she even mentioned it. I was astounded that she had never told me about her famous uncle but in retrospect it made sense. Roberta had a rare appreciation for the present, long before the billion-dollar industry of mindfulness research emerged. This was just one of her many personality traits that made me love her so much in the years we spent together in that 8' × 12' hot, little kitchen, laughing and cooking up a storm.

Sam was an ardent Roberta fan as well. Most mornings, he wandered into the tea room kitchen about the time she was taking freshly baked wine muffins from the oven. Roberta would then "butter him up," literally, not figuratively, with two or three hot ones, placing them in a little brown sack to take to the vineyard for him and Jack to snack on later in the morning. One day Sam was in the kitchen when Roberta mentioned there had been some recent break-ins in her neighborhood in Mound Bayou.

"Three of the houses on my street have been broken into the past two weeks," she said. "I just don't know what to do about it. I don't want to get a dog—I'm gone all day—but I may have to."

Roberta had been widowed quite a few years earlier, and her children had moved away to pursue their careers. She lived alone.

"You know, Roberta, I might have just the thing for you," Sam told her. "Be right back." The screen door slammed as he scurried out of the kitchen.

"Oh Lord," she muttered. "I hope Sam isn't bringing me a puppy."

A minute or two later, he was back, holding some sort of catalog in his hand. He had found the page he was looking for and spread it out on the counter.

"Here it is, Bert," Sam said. "Check this out. I just read about it yesterday and I think it's just the ticket for you."

The item he pointed to was the picture of a little black box with a mean dog, teeth bared, etched on the top. The three of us studied the description together. "Worried about break-ins? Can't get a dog? We can help!" The pitch went on to describe an apparatus one hooked up to a motion detector hanging on the outside doorknob. If someone jiggled it, the sensor would trigger the machine just inside the door. Then the poor sucker would be subjected to ferocious growls and barks emanating from the other side, undoubtedly scaring the bejesus out of him.

Roberta loved it. "I want me one of those," she told Sam. He pretty much did whatever she asked, so about a week later, he walked in with her brand new "Man's Best Friend" electronic dog. She named it Sparky. She soon had it all rigged up and never told a soul in the neighborhood about her "fake dog." When people heard the vicious barking, she just told them to wait on the porch while she put him in the back room.

Roberta never had trouble with trespassers after she acquired Sparky. When we closed the tea room many years later, he was still by her side, faithful as ever. "And the best thing about Sparky is," she loved to say, "you don't have to feed him."

One afternoon at the end of the day as we were counting the money in the tip jar, usually around forty or fifty dollars, Roberta remarked that she liked the cash tips she received every day much more than her weekly paycheck. Of course, the checks were considerably larger, but they were used for such mundane expenses as food and shelter. From the first day, we had a little blue and white teapot sitting by the cash box. We never had a cash register and credit card charges were processed by the old carbon slide gadget the bank provided. As we cleared the tables and collected the tips, we put every penny into the tea pot. When the last dish was put away and the floors swept, we all sat together around a table with a glass of iced tea and counted it. Then we divided it exactly four ways, between the two ladies in the kitchen and the two out front.

That was the money that the four of us loved the most, because we felt as though we could spend it any way we wanted. We all understood Roberta's appreciation of cash tips, a rare perk in such hard economic times. It made us feel sort of important, sort of white collar. Still, I carefully reported these tips on the W-2 forms each year, as IRS audits of small businesses loomed much larger in those days than they do today, especially in the Delta. Many people don't know this, but even now, eight of the top ten most audited counties in the United States are in Mississippi, and most of those are in the Delta. The average income of these counties is about $24,000 per year.

The only thing that seemed remotely déclassé about the tea room was the kitchen; nothing about it was commercial grade. We cooked on an old four-burner gas stove with the blackened oven below. We had a standard household refrigerator in the kitchen, which was supplemented by another, plus a freezer, in the wine lab. A microwave oven was mounted over an eight-foot counter where the plates were filled with food I often described as *gour-comf*, a word I coined early on to describe the unique fare at Top of the Cellar. Above were shelves of McCarty pottery. The kitchen also had a standard size dishwasher where we loaded the plates, cups, and glasses. The pots and pans had to be washed by hand.

One morning during that first year, a portly man appeared on the back doorstep, introducing himself as the state food inspector. That was one of the most frightening days I experienced at the tea room. He came unannounced, and when Roberta realized who he was and, more importantly, saw the horrified look on my face upon learning his identity, she took it upon herself to do the honors of showing him the setup. While our kitchen was spotless, it screamed "shoestring." The inspector made notes as he looked about the tiny kitchen, punctuating his examination of our poorly equipped kitchen with an occasional, ominous, "Hmmm . . ."

Finally, he put his clipboard in his briefcase and began to outline all the expensive upgrades we needed to make, from a new ventilation system to a complete water heater overhaul. I sensed that Roberta was close to running him off with the broom she held in her hand. But instead, as he completed his recitation, she looked at him and calmly asked, "Mister, do you really think we can afford to purchase all these upgrades? Do you think we don't *want* them?" I stood by with my mouth open as she rebuked the inspector for what could only be described as doing his job.

Then she paused, a slow smile spreading across her lovely face. "I'll tell you what," she said sweetly. I remember thinking, *Oh hell, what is she fixing to say . . . .*

"Why don't you hang around for lunch today and then tell us what we need to do?" She said this just as she was strategically pulling out a fresh, hot blackberry cobbler from the oven. Watching her, he immediately agreed to her terms.

Two hours later, the Northern Sector Food Inspector from the Great State of Mississippi was leaving through the back door of the tea room, heartily thanking us all for the wonderful lunch, gratis of course. Roberta put the broom back in the corner and we never heard from him, or any other state inspector, again.

Working in the kitchen alongside Roberta and me every morning was Florence. Flo was much younger than Roberta, but they had been good friends for years. Her boundless energy and sense of humor kept us hopping. Like Roberta, she was an integral part of the finely tuned workings of the kitchen. I quickly discovered that when Flo was there, I could forget about setting the kitchen timer because she had an internal clock in her head that knew, to the minute, when something needed to come out of the oven. As most in the restaurant business can tell you, servers paradoxically do their job most efficiently when they are absolutely slammed. And it seemed the slower things were in the dining room, the less likely it was that Shirley and I were taking care of business. It was Flo who often reminded us, "Y'all need to hush now and get on back out there," when we were all nibbling on leftovers and lost in conversation.

Shirley worked the front with me once the customers began arriving each day. She was responsible for making the wine muffins every morning, then moving on to the dining room to set the tables, polish the glasses, and post the menu on the little chalkboard in the main room. In her early twenties, Shirley was stunning, tall, and slim with curly blonde hair falling to her waist. She was a nursing student at nearby Delta State and a straight-A student. And Lord, was she fun to work with. Our customers, many of whom had known her since birth, appreciated her sharp wit, knowledge of everything Delta, and reliably sunny disposition. With Roberta, Flo, and Shirley around, it was hard not to love working at Top of the Cellar.

At the other end of the gravel road was where the heart of our lives, our children, spent their long days. Olivia had entered the family scene a decade or so earlier, before they were born, when Sam and I hired her as our housekeeper. Over the years, Liv evolved into the soul of our home—babysitter, cook, spiritual advisor, and housekeeper. That word, housekeeper —who do I think I am kidding here? Certainly no one from the Delta. The denigrating label most of us assigned the irreplaceable, much-loved Livs of our lives was "the maid," or maybe "the help," but never the more dignified title of "housekeeper." I am sorry to say that I was as guilty of this as anyone. For years I never questioned this ubiquitous noun choice, or the dubious rationale behind use of such an antiquated term. Despite the label, everyone knew that the strong and talented women who came into our homes to care for our children and tend to our households were much more than maids. They were often our teachers and mentors.

Black or white, Delta women remind me of the warning on a vehicle's side mirror: They are often closer, and larger, than they appear. Whatever illusion of them one likes to entertain—agreeable, malleable, fragile creatures, and so on—is pure drivel. Because farming is hard, dangerous work, many of the men are driven to early graves, which means women own most of the vast acreage of rich farmland left behind. And in the Delta, (s)he who has land, has power. As an eighty-year-old farmer's widow once explained to me in her soft, Southern drawl, "You know, Di, the women in the Delta are quite powerful." She smiled mischievously, leaned over, and quietly added, "After all, we have 80 percent of the land and 100 percent of the . . . well, the feminine wiles."

Women from this area have wielded their power since birth, generally using this force for good by paying it forward. Despite its steady position on the bottom rungs of the US economic ladder, Mississippi is always near the very top of the nation's list for charitable contributions to worthy organizations—local, national, and international alike. Giving is a way of life there and has been for generations. It is a trait to be proud of.

Liv was in her sixties when she came to work for us. She, her husband, and her son owned a farm east of Mound Bayou, where they planted and harvested beans and cotton, year after year. This farm was Liv's greatest source of pride, and understandably so. Small farms were disappearing quickly as the corporate agricultural wave swept across the Delta. Their farm was located a few miles east of Mound Bayou, and besides the crops, they also raised quite a few hogs and chickens, plus a killer vegetable garden. Liv often brought us fresh tomatoes, onions, and other heavenly produce, usually picked that morning.

"Y'all are gonna love what I got in my bag today!" Liv often said as she walked in the front door. Then she would open a brown grocery sack and pour out a bushel of crisp green beans or new potatoes onto the kitchen counter. She knew those were my favorite. After work, I would find her in her favorite chair in the living room, white apron spread across her knees, stringing the beans for supper while Lizzie and Matt "helped" as they watched cartoons.

At first, before the kids came along, Liv worked for us on Fridays only. That was the best day of the week for Sam and me, because we came home after a long day at the winery to find fried pork chops, mashed potatoes, hot cornbread, and a plethora of fresh vegetables, all cooked to perfection. Friday nights meant crisp, clean sheets on our bed—Liv preferred the clothesline to the dryer—and clean clothes neatly folded in the drawers. Some people outside the South believe that these incredible perks in life must have been unique to the affluent, but that was certainly not the case. I think it is safe to say that from the 1940s until near the end of the century, more than half of the white population in the Delta had housekeepers at least one day a week, regardless of their income level. These services were affordable because of the absurd wages for which these fine women were accustomed to working, and I am not proud of my benefitting from the system as I did, as a child and as an adult. Liv assured me many times that working for us was the best job she ever had, and that may have been true. I certainly hope that was the case. That said, I never let myself forget that the bar was mighty low.

Many years later, when Lizzie applied to law school at American University in DC, one of the questions on her application was, "What made you become interested in Human Rights Law?" Her response was an honest recap of some of her childhood conversations with Liv, who was always gentle, but candid about the injustice of her station in life. Lizzie was accepted.

Sam's and my challenges, on the other hand, were mostly minor ones, ranging from the mildly irritating, such as the air conditioner in the kitchen rattling, to the more serious, such as the real struggle in the slow winter season to pay the wages of our employees. Somehow, we always managed to keep everyone on full payroll, even on those days when we had more employees than customers darken our doors. Despite the trappings, Sam and I were far from wealthy, establishing a unique business in what was then, and still is, one of the poorest counties in the United States. But we always had hopes and dreams and a vision for something better down the road. We enjoyed the undying support of loyal customers and employees who were behind us from beginning to end, and we took so many things for granted.

For many in the Delta, however, Black or white, there was little hope. There were few realistic dreams. Wrapped up in my own life, I was clueless to the real challenges most people faced every day. And until the day I die, I will always admonish myself, not for the things I did, but for the many things I did not.

We are all the products of our time and place, some for the better, others for the worse. The Mississippi Delta is often described as "the most Southern place on earth." To some, this is a tribute, to others, not so much.

CHAPTER 6

A Brush of Conscience

November 4, 1979
Dixie Magazine—*Times-Picayune*
New Orleans, Louisiana
Muscadine Winery a Mississippi First
By Carolyn Thornton

. . . How did a Southern Baptist boy from Greenville, Miss. become interested in winemaking? Well, Rushing and his wife, Diane, spent (time) in the German town of Ansbach while he was in the service. Their love for wines dates from that period.

When they returned to the States, they both went back to school, and Rushing received his agricultural degree from Mississippi State University at about the time a native wine law was passed in Mississippi.

. . . Diane laughed as the cocker spaniel, Ansbach, came into the room. "We have varying degrees of sophistication in our control," she said. Pointing to Ansbach, she explained, "He came into the tasting room drunk as a skunk one day. I went over and smelled his breath. It was Rushing Red. But I didn't know where he had gotten it. In the back of the cellar I found a tank that was dripping. He saved us several thousand dollars, because it would have literally gone down the drain if he hadn't gotten so drunk." (Their cat nips a little, too, Diane admitted, but knows when to stop.)

"Y'all grew up in Greenville, didn't you?" asked the sheriff as we followed the winding brick sidewalk through the flower beds back towards the winery. Stopping at the mound above the wine cellar, Sam pointed out the dark red thread of wine slowly trickling from the cellar drainpipe down the hill and into the Sunflower. It was surreal to watch. "And didn't you go to State?" he continued. I could tell he was trying to take our minds off the macabre scene that lay before us.

"Yes, Sir," I said, wondering what difference any of this made at all, but automatically going along with the pretext. "We've known each other since the fourth grade," I added, for what reason I do not know. But sometimes longevity in a relationship translates to stability, and I was grasping at any constant at this point. Because until that point, my life had been nothing if not stable.

The first time I laid eyes on Sam was when I was nine years old. We were in elementary school in Greenville, Mississippi, when he, as the esteemed President of the Matty Akin Student Body, led us in "a word of prayer" before the school assembly each week. We continued in the same schools through graduation and even went to the same church. But we didn't really pay much attention to each other until my sophomore year in high school, 1968. We dated on and off that year, but other love interests took us both elsewhere until my freshman year in college.

I remember the day well. My best friend Jackie and I were doing the loop on Washington and Main in Greenville on a Sunday afternoon, a considerable source of entertainment for my generation back then. We were stopped at a red light near everyone's favorite hangout, Strazi's Drive In. Windows down, we were tuned in to music on my eight-track tape player. Sam pulled up in his green MGB convertible in the lane beside us, looked over, and asked what we were listening to. Music blared from his little car as well. It turned out we were both listening to Pink Floyd's "Careful with That Axe, Eugene." It was an absurdly serendipitous moment for both of us. I had just finished my first semester at Millsaps College, a small liberal arts school in

Jackson, and I was in the process of transferring to Ole Miss. I had decided I wasn't "disciplined enough" (read: smart enough) to go to Millsaps. Sam was a sophomore at Mississippi State but was not exactly thriving either, academically at least—too many distractions, he vaguely claimed. Recognizing a mutual respect for the wonders of Pink Floyd, we began dating again. After he confessed one night that I made his socks roll up and down, we became inseparable.

To make a long story short, Sam's poor performance at State and a low draft number resulted in his being inducted into the Army in the waning days of the Vietnam War. Instead of being sent to Southeast Asia, however, he ended up as a clerk in the Bavarian town of Ansbach, Germany. It seems Sam's penchant for pretty girls had saved him from the conflict. When he was about sixteen, he had noticed that all the lovely young ladies at Greenville High School took typing class, so he also signed up. He was the only boy in a class of thirty or so. A few years later when he was drafted and subsequently tested, he was the best typist in the large batch of draftees. This resulted in his being assigned a clerkship in Europe instead of a gun in Vietnam.

After settling into his barracks in Ansbach, Sam immediately began his campaign to marry me and bring me over. He had already laid the groundwork before he left by going to my father's office one afternoon the summer before and asking for my hand in marriage. The plan at the time was for us to get married as soon as Sam got out of the army, two years and some change later.

"Mornin', Mr. Paul," Sam began as they shook hands firmly. He had worn a coat and tie for the occasion. He knew that my father was a clothes horse who firmly embraced the Shakespearian sentiment, "Apparel oft proclaims the man." He told me later that he could tell that Daddy knew why he had come by the look on his face.

"I've come to ask you if I can marry your daughter," Sam said bravely. "I want you to know I love her, and I will take good care of her."

"Well, Sam, I thought that might be why you were here," my father responded, in his slow, deliberate style. A frequent golfer, my father sported a deep tan on his round, bald head. He told anyone who was interested that God had made very few perfect heads, and the rest He had covered with hair. He was very persuasive. Fortunately for Sam, Daddy had known him for many years and liked him. Rex Paul smiled, leaned back in his chair and studied Sam for a moment, smoke curling from the cigarette in his right hand. "I will give y'all my blessing under one condition," he said.

Sam waited, wondering if he would be able to meet it. He knew it was important, and it was.

Daddy took a final drag off his cigarette and snuffed it out in the crystal ashtray on his desk. Leaning forward, he said, "First you have to promise me that Diane will finish her college education."

Sam related the entire conversation that evening as we celebrated with a bottle of Ripple on the levee in Greenville, where everyone "parked" in those days. Daddy had gone on to say that because Pearl Harbor had been attacked in the middle of his sophomore year in college, he had been unable to finish his last two years. By the time the war ended in 1945, he had a wife and their first baby on the way. I knew that this had always nagged at him. In later years, he would tease that although he was "the least-educated person in this family," he was still the boss. My father valued education more than anyone I have ever known. Sam said he knew that he was perfectly serious and would certainly hold him to his word. I have no doubt that he was right. None of us knew, however, that the plan would advance so quickly, skipping a couple of years.

By then I was a sophomore English major at Ole Miss, a much better fit for my academic and social temperament. The University of Mississippi is located in Oxford, Mississippi, a beautiful old town featuring many antebellum homes. There I studied hard and partied harder. The 'rents paid extra for me to have a private dorm room, and it quickly became the party spot for the girls on the tenth floor at "New Dorm." Music ranging from Joni Mitchell to Jimi Hendrix boomed from my room every night; fortunately, the RA was one of us, so no problem there. Mama had been a Kappa Kappa Gamma at the University of Arkansas, making me a "legacy," so I was invited to the Kappa house for dinner a few times my first semester at Ole Miss. The food there was a big improvement over the grilled cheese sandwiches from the vending machines in the basement of the dorm, and the girls were nice. Still, I didn't see it as a particularly good return on my investment, so I eventually told them I just wasn't interested. I had already made great friends by then, most of them from the Gulf Coast.

Of course, co-ed dorms were unheard of back then, at least in the Deep South. When fathers or brothers entered the hallways to help us move in or move out, one always heard, "Man in the hall!" echo loudly down the corridor, hurrying towel-clad girls back to the communal showers. Although I am usually first in the queue for societal change, I don't think I would have enjoyed living with guys next door to me in the dorm. Running up and down the hallway in our shortie pajamas with orange juice cans in our hair is one of my best memories of my days at Ole Miss.

Sam completed his basic training in Louisiana and was shipped overseas just after the Christmas holidays in January 1973. He officially proposed from Germany about six weeks later on Valentine's Day, and the art of the proposal should have been an indicator of the unpredictability that was to follow. Back then, long distance calls were expensive. Those were the days when one telephoned one's grandma for no more than seven minutes during a specific window of time on Sunday evenings so as not to be surprised by a nasty phone bill at the end of the month. Therefore, Sam's Valentine's Day marriage proposal from Europe had to be quick and efficacious for economic reasons, factors not conducive to what should have been one of the most romantic moments of our lives.

Adding to this stressful enterprise was the fact that since he was calling from overseas, Sam had to participate in an elaborate dance unique to time and place. First, he had to go to the Ansbach post office and stand in line for thirty minutes to speak with an elderly man who knew no English; Germany was, after all, another country.

This was required to reserve a time to call the States, a time that had to be at least ten days out so that Sam could write and tell me when to be in my dorm room to take the call. Next, he had to speculate/relate/translate how long the call would last and get in another line to pay for that predetermined time, which cost about $80 for the three minutes he purchased. His last requirement, ten days later, was to show up, and he's always been good at that.

While we had been writing letters to each other daily, we had not talked on the phone in over a month, so there was a bit of catching up to do. I don't think it takes much of an imagination to see where this is going; less than a second after he nervously asked me to marry him, our prepaid allotted time was up and we were disconnected. The next week, I accepted Sam's marriage proposal via airmail. He celebrated my response a week later with his army buddies in Germany while I celebrated in a similar manner with my girlfriends in the dorm. I'm pretty sure alcohol was involved at both locations. I just loved being "educated at Oxford."

Sam came home in June, and our first order of business was to pick out wedding rings. I didn't have an engagement ring and honestly did not care whether I got one or not. As we stood at a discount jewelry store reviewing our options, I knew they were limited when his eyes went straight to the "Simple Gold Rings" display. Glancing at the diamond rings in the next case, he asked somewhat seriously if I would rather have an engagement ring or a refrigerator. I told him when we got back from Germany, we would likely need the refrigerator more, so we purchased the simple gold bands that still grace our third fingers today. Mine cost $29.95 and his was $34.95. They have held up nicely over the years, a lot longer than the refrigerator did.

The large wedding was held on June 9 at the First Baptist Church in Greenville, a huge, beautiful church we had both attended since elementary school. I didn't care very much about the wedding details, which is why it was about as unimaginative as a wedding can be. It began with the vapid "Here Comes the Bride" and was followed by an uninspiring ceremony conducted by the pastor. I remember the prewedding conference when Sam and I met with the Rev. Landry. I shook the good reverend up a little when I insisted he take out the bit about my promising to "obey." Sam knew that was a nonstarter for me from the get-go, but it appeared to come as somewhat of a shock to the preacher.

The only memorable feature of our big day was that it was the first time that Black people other than "the family maid" had been invited as guests to a wedding at that church. My good friends, Janis and Iris, went to Greenville High School, then Millsaps in Jackson, as I had. We were friendly enough in high school, but we really bonded in college. Every evening I would make my way down the hall to their dorm room, and we would listen to music and talk for hours. Many of our dorm mates had a hard time telling these beautiful sisters apart, as they were identical twins. But to me it was easy—most of the time, Janis wore her hair straight while Iris preferred an Afro. Their father was a civil rights activist, which is likely why his daughters were among the first Black students to attend an all-white school in Greenville.

They were just tiny girls in the seventh grade when Janis and Iris first walked up the white marble steps at E. E. Bass Junior High School. I attended a different school across town, so I didn't meet them until we were in high school, but I can imagine the hardships they faced. I can imagine them because we had our first Black student, Gail, at Solomon Jr. High that same year. Iris and Janis were two of a very small handful of Black people at E. E. Bass; Gail was the only Black student in our school of more than seven hundred. I can still envision her carefully navigating the crowded hallways at our brand-new school, alone, her books tightly clutched to her chest. Tall and graceful, she looked like a queen.

Until one day that fall of 1965, I thought of myself as a nice twelve-year-old, quite enlightened in view of the fact that I had grown up a privileged white girl in the Mississippi Delta. I knew better than to use the "N-word" and felt, for the most part, that Black people had gotten a bad rap. Also, I had come to believe that being a racist was not cool. I had helped Gail with her combination lock the first day of school and shown her where to get her lunch ticket punched in the cafeteria. I had even been the first one to drink after her at the water fountain by home room class. Yep, I felt pretty good about my sanctimonious little self. But when I found myself in the girls' locker room at Solomon that day, looking into Gail's dark, questioning eyes, I knew I had been deluding myself all along.

"Ten laps and then to the showers!" the gym teacher shouted. God, how I hated her voice. In fact, I hated everything about P.E. class, from the agony of undressing in front of my classmates to the icy cold showers that awaited us afterwards. The room always smelled of dirty socks, and it was not uncommon for one of the boys to open the door wide enough to expose all of us partially clad tweens to gawking faces peering in for a quick thrill, prompting peels of ear-piercing screams. The whole concept was primitive as far as I was concerned, and I could not imagine why some ancient administrator had deemed it necessary to include physical education in the academic curriculum. Adding further insult, all of us were required to wear one-piece white uniforms for gym class. The condition of these hideous hot-pants-hybrids soon became a subtle reflection of our home life, as we had to take them home to launder them ourselves. Some of the girls took theirs every day and returned the next with starched, blindingly white uniforms; others didn't wash theirs for weeks.

Standing at the mirrors brushing my hair, I watched in the reflection as Gail, The Black Girl, sat alone in the locker cubicle, slowly tying her immaculate white tennis shoe in a safety knot. Her grandmother had probably taught her the same survival skill that mine had, double tying one's shoestring to prevent its coming loose and tripping one up, heaven forbid. Standing back up, she began looking through her small purse for something. I couldn't help but admire her natural grace, her slow, deliberate moves, and cool aloofness. From what source of strength did this young girl draw her courage, I wondered. What could make a beautiful Black girl want to leave the school that had elected her the "Class Favorite" to come and put up with the bullshit this school dished out to her every day? Damned if I understand it, I thought.

"Diane, I can't find my hairbrush . . . Do you think I could borrow yours?"

The room became deathly silent as about fifteen girls stood frozen in place. Gail was asking to use my brush? She rarely spoke to anyone, including me. Tammy, a vulgar blonde girl in our class and a known troublemaker, was looking at me with an ugly "You wouldn't dare!" glare.

I turned to Gail, trying hard to mask my surprise. "Sure, here." I quickly handed her the brush and pretended to be busy with my books. I sensed, rather than saw, the girls slowly resume their activity in low whispering voices that must be, I decided, what Hell sounds like.

"You ain't gonna let her use your hairbrush, are you?" Tammy asked in a loud, abrasive tone. She looked over at Gail, studying her from head to toe. "I sure wouldn't."

I looked at Tammy's reflection in the mirror in front of me and answered, "Yes." I didn't dare say more. Tammy could be a formidable foe. Just the week before she had threatened a friend of mine who had helped Gail pick up a book she had dropped in the hallway.

Gail lowered the hairbrush and looked at me. I slowly lifted my eyes into large brown ones that spoke courage and guarded friendliness. I could tell she was interested in how this would go down. She didn't seem frightened, just intrigued by the tense exchange between this dreadful girl and me. She studied me for a moment as she held the brush, a question in her eyes, one that was centuries old, as old as mankind's first injustice. I knew what she was asking, and it was for a lot more than a hairbrush. I failed her miserably as I stood there, saying nothing more in response to Tammy's vile comment. She didn't say a word as she handed it back to me.

"I'd throw that brush in the trash if I was you," Tammy snorted. "It ain't no use to nobody now." She looked at me, then Gail, and swaggered to the swinging door that led to the gymnasium. Her hand on the door, she looked back at me and snickered.

"Pussy," she said, laughing as she passed through the opening.

The only sound in the locker room was the distant reverberation of basketballs slapping the gymnasium floors. A few seconds later, I regained my composure, ostensibly at least.

"Sorry 'bout that," I said to Gail, avoiding her eyes as I tucked the brush back into my purse.

"It's okay," she said. Then she picked up her things and sat on the bench nearby, waiting for the rest of us to move on.

I wish that I could report that I had been chastened by the shameful conduct that went down that afternoon at Solomon Jr. High, but that would be deceitful and self-serving. Instead, as I flew out of the girls' locker room that cool fall day, I was mad—mad at Tammy for being such a despicable creep, mad at Gail for putting me in that position, and mad at myself for being such a coward. Yet, despite the loud parade of angry thoughts marching through my head, I was chiefly struck by the dignity with which Gail had handled the situation.

That night at home, I revisited the scene over and over in my head as I sat alone in my baby blue bedroom, adorned with posters of a new band called The Beatles. As I rolled my hair on pink foam curlers, I thought about the look on Gail's face when I didn't stand up for her. I entertained as many justifications for my cowardice as I could think of, but in the end, I was just ashamed of myself. It took a few days for me to work out why Gail didn't seem as shaken as I was when Tammy confronted us—she had remained unflappable throughout the entire episode. I concluded later that week it was because to her, this sordid encounter was nothing new—just the status quo. The thought was sobering.

For the next three years, I never partook in the verbal abuse Gail was subjected to from time to time at school, but I didn't come to her defense either. Very few did. I greeted her in the halls every day, and I was always polite. I would help her with a problem in math class or she would help me with a concept in science. But I never went out of my way to make her feel included, even though I liked her very much.

Gail stayed at Solomon all three years and to this day, I don't know how she persevered. Things for her seemed to ease a bit when we entered high school, as she rejoined friends from her elementary school days. She was elected "Most Beautiful" at Greenville High when we were seniors, which pleased me to no end. Janis and Iris run into Gail from time to time, as they all three live in Greenville now. I would love to see her again, but I am not sure I have the courage; the locker room incident and what it told me about my white, fragile self is still too depressing. But I am working on it.

CHAPTER 7

A Precarious Solidarity

November 7, 2016
The Nation www.thenation.com
From: The Hechinger Report
The Anonymous Town That Was the Model
of Desegregation in the Civil-Rights Era
By LynNell Hancock

GREENVILLE, Miss.—They called it "River City," singled out half a century ago as a beacon of hope for school integration in the South. Authors of the landmark civil rights-era Coleman Report, a massive federal survey of U.S. educational inequality, concluded that if desegregation were to work anywhere in the Deep South, it would be in this town, an oasis of tolerance and pragmatic gentility in the Mississippi Delta, the blackest, poorest, "most southern place on earth."

Neva Elizabeth Paul, my mother, was the only Special Education teacher at Greenville High School when we all transitioned there in 1968 for our sophomore year. Each year, she taught about twenty students in a hot, un-air-conditioned trailer behind the gym; sadly, this was the norm back then. Mama was known throughout the school for her compassion and considerable skill in working with her students. She started the Vocational-Technical Program for Special

Education in Greenville, and years later, many of her students were still working at the same jobs she had secured for them in high school. Often during supper that year, Mama asked how Iris and Janis were getting along, as she liked and respected the twins very much.

When Janis visited me in Colorado in 2004, she and I went over one morning to check on Mama, who had turned 89 the year before. She had moved to Ouray six years earlier after Daddy died, and she had grown to love the little mountain town as much as we did. She lived in her own small house on the other side of Main Street, where the "Red-Light District" had been located a hundred years before during Ouray's raucous mining days. She loved to tell everyone who visited that she felt more at home on that side of town.

As we sat in her living room, Mama asked about Janis's family. She was acquainted with her father, as he had been our mail carrier in Greenville for years. She laughed as she told Janis that the only Christmas present my father had personally purchased every year was a bottle of good bourbon for Mr. Moore. He would stick it in the mailbox, where he promptly received a sincere thank-you note the next day. She also knew the twins' aunt, Mrs. Haynes, who had been my English teacher during senior year. I remember passing the teacher's lounge every day at school, cigarette smoke pouring out the door, watching them chatting away. Mama told Janis as we were leaving that day that those years she spent teaching at Greenville High had been among her finest, because they had required the best of everyone, striving to make things work during turbulent times.

Janis and Iris also became successful teachers, Iris working in Greenville and Janis in Los Angeles. When we are together these days, the three of us sometimes talk of our experiences in the late sixties and early seventies. We appreciate the historical significance of those rocky days, and speak of memories, good and bad, with candor. Predictably, our recollections of those times often don't match up.

A diverse city—home to Black, white, Chinese, Jewish, Italian, and Lebanese people, to name a few—Greenville had been the first city in Mississippi to defy the governor and offer "freedom of choice" for all races to attend their school of preference in the midsixties. That was when Janis, Iris, Gail, and a few other Black students entered the white schools for the first time. But a new federal ruling in the summer of 1970 was a game-changer for everyone. Over the summer, the Black high school, Coleman, was converted to a middle school, sending all its juniors and seniors to Greenville High, which we attended. The other Black secondary school, T. L. Weston, became home to all the sophomores in the district. Overnight, the historic Coleman High School was, quite simply, no more.

That fall, "White Flight" in Greenville captured headlines across the nation. Tiny private schools in Greenville increased in enrollment as hundreds of Black students entered our doors for the first time. It was interesting to watch as students who had been in public schools with us since the first grade suddenly disappeared from our hallways. We knew that many of the fifteen percent or so whites who left that first year did so reluctantly, their parents fearing what the new paradigm might mean for them. Those of us who stayed were, for the most part, either the children of the more open-minded in the community or the children of those who couldn't afford private schools.

The prospect of my leaving Greenville High was never broached with my parents. It was a given that I would remain at the school where my mother taught and where I thrived. I am profoundly grateful that I stayed; my senior year turned out to be a gratifying journey of questions asked, lessons learned, and relationships built. I think most of the students that year felt as I did, that it largely fell to us to make this new model for education work for everyone. More importantly, most of us sincerely wanted it to work. We sensed, correctly, that the entire nation was watching us. As the years went by, however, the percentage of whites leaving the public schools increased dramatically. As Hancock stated in her article published in *The Nation* (cited above) forty-five years later, "By all accounts, if the adults had left the children of Greenville alone, integration might have survived." True, that.

The introduction to our senior yearbook, the 1971 *Vespa* captured it well. Written by classmate and editor Maury Elizabeth McGough, it reads:

> In the summer of 1970, the Federal Courts ruled that all Greenville Public Schools completely desegregate. Greenville High became the school for all eleventh and twelfth graders in the Greenville Separate School District. Thus, three high schools merged into one.
>
> . . . September 7, 1970 was set aside for discussion in every class about the new, unitary situation. Most students felt that communication and cooperation were the most important factors in helping GHS run smoothly. Many also felt that students still identified with their old schools, but others thought that the band and team sports would help bring about unity at GHS.
>
> . . . Students were challenged to mature physically, mentally, and socially. In the process of this growth, during one short year, came the realization that theirs was the world to challenge. Drugs, the Vietnam War, pollution, the Middle East Conflict, unemployment— these were no longer separated from the students' world, but were now a vital challenge to their security, especially since eighteen-year-olds obtained the right to vote.

Coleman High School had been a football and basketball powerhouse for many years, often taking the state title. It was also renowned throughout the state as a good school academically. It was established in the 1920s at a time when fewer than a third of Black children made it past fifth grade, having to work in the cotton fields instead. Still, it was never discussed which of the two mascots, the GHS Hornets or the Coleman Tigers, would survive the upheaval. The talented Coleman athletes who had worked so hard were forced to give up their accolades as well as their mascot. When the doors opened in the fall of 1970, the Coleman athletic trophies did not grace the showcase at the entrance, as did those from GHS. Nor did the framed Certificates of Academic Excellence. When Janis pointed this out decades later, I admitted I had never even thought about that. I guess that pretty much sums up the problem.

This is just one of many inequities that were revealed to me in my later years, sometimes by friends, other times in history books. It wasn't until Janis and Iris visited Sam and me in 2016 that I learned of another, much more personal one. The three of us were sharing a bottle of Pinot Grigio in my living room, sitting in our pajamas and reminiscing. Somehow, the subject of my wedding came up. That's when they told me that one of our ushers had refused to seat them when they first arrived at the church. Fortunately, another had quickly stepped forward, averting a scene. Both added that everyone else there had welcomed them, telling them how happy they were to see them there on our big day. Iris then confided that their father had been reluctant to let them come, fearing a reprisal of some sort, and the three of them had discussed the matter at length. But he had ultimately left the decision to them.

In a never-ending affirmation of personal cluelessness, I was genuinely shocked by these revelations. I apologized repeatedly, assuring Janis and Iris that I had known nothing about the underlying angst brought down on them by my invitation. In their typically kind fashion, they told me I was too hard on myself, that it was new for everyone back then. I apologized to them one last time anyway, knowing I was about forty-three years late.

CHAPTER 8

Business 101: How to Work at a Real Job

September 1, 1978
The Reflector
Mississippi State University
Starkville, Mississippi
Former MSU students own state's only commercial winery
By Marsh Nichols, Editor

There's a touch of the "Old World" tucked away in the Mississippi Delta. The Winery Rushing, located three miles east of Merigold, north of Cleveland, has mixed European processes with redneck intuition to produce the state's first commercial wine in the state since Prohibition.

And, with the exception of stomping their own grapes, the team of Sam and Diane Rushing produce four varieties of wine "in the traditional European way," going as far as racking their wine during its aging tenure.

The young couple first became interested in the wine business shortly after they were married five years ago. Sam was paying his dues to Uncle Sam in Ansbach, Germany, and, during that one-and-a-half year hitch, he and Diane visited various wineries located about two hours from the U.S. post.

"We never, at that time, halfway imagined we'd end up owning and producing our own wine though," Diane said.

Three days after the wedding, Sam and I flew to Bavaria. I had never held a "real" job, had been north of Tennessee once, and had never been on a plane in my life. Germany was magical to me, and I was soon enthralled with my new husband and tiny apartment. Our first place was on the third floor over a butcher shop in Ansbach, located in the Franconia region of Bavaria. In 2017, when we revisited the town with some old friends who had been stationed there with us, the shop was still in business at #9 Johann Sebastian Bach Platz.

Kandert Metzgerei was a fine little meat market run by two generations of the Kandert family. It had been there for many years and was of excellent repute. While our only contact with Herr and Frau Kandert was on the first of each month when we paid the rent, we could see and hear them work in the inner courtyard below our bedroom window. Each morning around five o'clock, Sam and I were awakened by the shriek of a pig or the screech of a chicken as it was being butchered. The terrible sounds were accentuated by the rusty odor of blood as it made its way through our open, lace-covered window. It was an unsettling way to start the day, but we quickly became accustomed to this ghastly alarm clock. Sunday mornings proved more pleasant, marked by the peel of church bells instead of the squeal of animals.

The building where the shop and our apartment were located was part of the ancient Ansbach palace wall. The butcher shop faced the commercial street, and our living room faced the old palace mews and grounds. The fragrances on that side of our little apartment were much more appealing. Every Saturday morning at the break of dawn, the farmers' market set up just below our living room window. I watched from the third floor as the immaculate little trucks unloaded crates of fresh vegetables, beautiful flowers, and hand-crafted candies. I was struck by their artistry in setting up the booths with their wares—the glossy, purple eggplants next to the bright green butter lettuce, baskets of ripe red tomatoes surrounded by perfect circles of white cauliflower. Each stand had its own shiny brass scale hanging from a pole to weigh the produce. After Deutsch marks traded hands, it was then placed in the shoppers' canvas bags and loaded into their ubiquitous rolling carts; these vendors and shoppers were "green" long before the world became savvy to the perils of plastic bags.

The flower stands were my favorite, filled with huge, dewy blossoms of plants I had never known existed. And everything was so fresh, likely picked early that very morning. From above, the market looked like little movie sets, each with its own decorated stage, colorful props, and animated cast of characters. It spread over the ancient cobblestones like a colorful quilt, reminiscent of scenes straight out of Shakespeare.

Even more intriguing than the bright displays, however, were the delightful locals who manned them. This barely-twenty-year-old bride who had been an entitled Ole Miss coed just a month earlier immediately fell in love with these merry, overall-clad farmers and their sassy wives. I remember sitting at the windowsill and studying the people below as they exchanged familiar, tribal quips while unloading their trucks, obviously old friends. Most of the women wore faded dresses covered by flowery aprons with large pockets. The farm families appeared to be multigenerational; the younger ones, many teenagers, were the picture of health with their tanned arms and rosy cheeks. They worked as hard as their elders but didn't seem quite as enamored by this centuries-old Saturday ritual as their parents and grandparents. This was the early seventies, and doubtless they were experiencing the same need to break from the old ways as did all those of our generation, regardless of the continent we called home. I am sure they wanted to wrap it up and enjoy the rest of their weekend, like young people everywhere. I envied them, though, for their strong familial ties and sense of purpose. I also fancied the girls' porcelain complexions, impossibly shiny hair and overall glow of health, a by-product of their organic diet and lifestyle no doubt.

Most of the older women in the community appeared on the street each day dressed in black dresses and kerchief head coverings.

Quite a few were marked with severely bowed legs, a legacy of early malnutrition stemming from having survived not one, but two world wars. Not surprisingly, there were many more old women than old men; this was, after all, only twenty-eight years after the second world war ended. The old men seemed more empowered somehow, happier, stronger. It was a strange juxtaposition of ethos these war survivors seemed to embrace, and I found the whole dynamic fascinating.

As soon as the market opened at seven a.m. each Saturday, I was there with my wicker basket and a few marks. Unable to speak the language, I usually just smiled and pointed at what I wanted. I quickly learned the difference between a gram and an ounce and how to communicate through pantomime. Never having been shy in my life, I had no aversion to making a complete fool of myself in order to get what I wanted. I often made animal sounds to be sure the meat was a proper cut and not an organ from some gruesome critter I had never heard of. On the occasions that I had to resort to such indignity, Sam would just wander away as though he didn't know me. But it was great fun for me as well as the farmers.

Our apartment's proximity to the Saturday market was a delightful surprise when I arrived, but we didn't live there for very long. Little did I know when I said yes to Sam's proposal that our apartment cost $320/month and Sam brought home just over $340. After a come-to-Jesus conversation or two, we wisely concluded two things: We had to find a cheaper place to live and I needed to get a job. The problem was I didn't speak a word of German.

After our fiscal epiphany, Sam and I sat down, split a bottle of Gewürztraminer, and discussed the likelihood of my finding employment. The prospects seemed dismal. As a draftee's wife, I was unlikely to find employment at Hindenburg Kaserne, the American base in the heart of town where Sam worked. We DWs were quite discriminated against in those days, often sent to the back of the line in the commissary if an officer's wife or "lifer brat" wanted to break in. I recall that once I had been sent to the back seven times when trying to buy a loaf of bread. At that point, I loudly denounced the entire charade as "unmitigated bullshit," and was asked to leave by the MPs.

Undeterred by total lack of marketable skills, however, the next day I scouted the beautiful midsize town of Ansbach until I happened upon a big factory just off the Promenade. It was surrounded by a tall fence, and to enter, I had to talk with one of the uniformed guards at the gate. It was a bit intimidating, to say the least. I walked up to the gate, pulled the little translation guide out of my purse, and haltingly told the guard, "Ich brauche arbeit," meaning "I need work." He snickered, opened the gate, and directed me to the office. Fortunately, one of the men in the office spoke a little English and with his help, I was able to fill out an application. I suppose they were in dire need of labor, as they hired me on the spot and told me I was to start the next day.

Very German, very austere, the Bosch Automotive Plant became my second home for the next ten months. I clocked in at seven a.m. each weekday and left the windowless factory nine hours later. For every minute we were late, we were docked one hour's pay. Most of those months it was dark when I went to work and dark when I got out. My task was on an assembly line where 3,200 times a day, I placed two little screws upside down on their heads on a plate and sent them on to the extremely loud press just two feet to my right. My supervisor scared the hell out of me the first few weeks with his patrolling the floor shouting "Macht schnell!" ("Go faster!") but eventually he warmed up to me. I had been working the line for six months before I had the courage to ask him what I was making, because my imagination had been overactive of late. I had recently reread Eisenhower's farewell speech of 1961 and had been speculating a bit about my part in perhaps unwittingly building an accoutrement that benefited the Industrial War Machine. So, I decided to ask exactly what it was that I was crafting every day. After gesticulating ourselves through the language barrier, it emerged that I was making an important part of the seat belt buzzer apparatus for Mercedes sports coupes. Or at least I think that's what he said.

The German girl who sat just to my left, Renata, remains my friend to this day; we still correspond at Christmas. She taught me quite a bit of German as we worked side by side for nearly a year. I have always been a talker, and since the only words she knew in English were, "I love you," I knew I needed to learn the language if I was going to have any fun at work. We talked all day long, haltingly at first, and I learned much about her growing up in Bavaria. She told me how, in her midteens, she, like most others, had failed the national test that would have enabled her to continue with high school. She had been working at Bosch ever since, along with girls from all over the world. I became fast friends with Sicilians, Turks, Greeks, and Yugoslavians, most of whom spoke neither German nor English. We would order our lunch each day from a little cart that wound its way through the factory and sit together near the line. I don't know how we communicated, but we found a way. Maybe it was because of the vending machine which offered a wonderful variety of German beers. It was plugged in at lunch time each day. I found it fascinating that there was absolutely no stigma attached to inserting a coin for a cold one during the middle of the workday at said place of work.

I was one of only two people from the US who worked in the large factory, and those were the days when American Exceptionalism was still a thing in Europe. I felt sort of like a movie star at times, as these ladies and I exchanged life stories. After the first conversation or two, however, I intuitively knew to tone down descriptions of the life I had led in America. These women were from countries that still had bullet holes in their buildings. Most had immigrated to Germany to work and send money home to their impoverished communities. Some of the stories were sad—a few of them had lived through the war—and the conversation was humbling to me. But most of the repartee was filled with laughter and the occasional, universally understood man-bashing.

As the days went by, I did more listening and less talking. We rattled on about everything under the sun, except for one: World

War II. I quickly learned that was one topic that was strictly ver-
boten. At first, I had tried to learn a little about its lasting effects
on my friends, but I was shut down very quickly. Once, however,
Renata asked if my father had fought in the war. I responded in the
affirmative and it seemed to make her sad. I knew that her father,
Fritz, had fought under Hitler. I recall the sense of relief on her face
when I immediately added that Daddy had served as a Navy pilot in
the Pacific theater. I think we were both glad of that. The possibility that our fathers had somehow crossed paths during that terrible
time was untenable.

I still enjoy practicing my German on my yearly visits to Europe
when I visit Lizzie, who lives in Geneva, Switzerland. I always try
to reconnect with a few folks there and frequent my old haunts,
especially some of the bars. Interestingly, I speak German best when
I'm a little drunk.

Soon after I began working at Bosch, we found a less expensive
flat in the tiny village of Burgoberbach, not too far from Ansbach.
Rent there was about $150/month, and while the place was immacu-
late and relatively new, it had no hot running water. We had to buy
Jimmy Dean charcoal at the commissary and build a fire under the
water tank any time we wanted to take a bath. The whole ordeal took
a couple of hours, but we adapted quickly. With another two hundred dollars, we bought a gray 1958 Volkswagen Bug, replete with its
little glass flower vase mounted by the windshield. I commented to
Sam that the previous owner must have glued it on, but he insisted
that it was standard on all the old VW models. He was right. I stuck
a yellow plastic daisy that had blown into our yard from the nearby
cemetery in there and called it good.

We became quite close with our landlords in Burgoberbach, Herr
and Frau Pfeiffer, and their thirteen-year-old daughter, Roswitha.
The Pfeiffers owned a shoe repair shop in Ansbach and enjoyed
a brisk business. He had been captured by Americans during the
conflict and shipped to the Navy base in Miami, where he bar-
tended until the end of the war. He liked Americans almost as

much as he liked Jim Beam whiskey, which he couldn't get on "the economy," as we called the German market. So, paying the rent on the first day of each month became a wonderful ritual of gifting Herr Pfeiffer a bottle of Jim Beam from the base commissary in addition to the rent. In turn, he "gifted" us with endless shots of Jägermeister schnapps, which invariably reduced both Sam and me to blubbering sentimentalists. Remarkably, I became quite fond of Jägermeister after that.

We visited the Pfeiffers on quite a few occasions after returning to the States, mostly in the 1980s and '90s. They remained like family to us until their deaths, and we still stay in touch with Roswitha and her wonderful husband Robert. They live in the same house where Sam and I lived nearly fifty years ago, although it has been renovated several times and is absolutely stunning now. We last visited them a few years ago and it was great to reconnect, as always. We ended the afternoon with a visit to the little cemetery on the edge of town to pay our respects to Herr and Frau Pfeiffer.

I am not a big proponent of aphorisms, but one that has always resonated with me is that "silver lining" thing. Despite Sam's vehement protest upon being drafted in 1972, even he will admit today it was one of the best things that ever happened to us. We learned a lot about ourselves that year in Germany. In fact, I am not altogether sure that our marriage would have survived had it not been for the thousands of miles and thousands of dollars that lay between me and my mama during that first year as newlyweds. We were very young, and we were very opinionated, both of us accustomed to getting our way. When we argued, which was often, I would wander to the nearby forest and feel sorry for myself for hours. I obsessed over the inequities of my life: I couldn't go home because I didn't have any money, and I couldn't talk to anyone about it because I didn't speak German. I wasn't even able to drive off in a huff because I had flunked my German driver's test. To make matters worse, I gained ten pounds that first month because all I knew how to cook was cake, macaroni and cheese, and baked beans.

One morning, about a week before I had secured my job on the assembly line, I woke up and decided that a good wife made cakes for her husband while he was at work. So, I headed over to the commissary on the base and bought a Betty Crocker cake mix and icing. It turned out to be very good, so good in fact that I decided to have a little piece before Sam got home that evening. By the time 5 o'clock rolled around, there was one tiny sliver remaining on the plate. I was physically miserable and terribly ashamed of myself. I began brainstorming "outs" to this situation, knowing that I couldn't claim that friends had come by and shared it with me because I didn't have any friends on the continent. Then I realized that Sam had no way of knowing that I had even baked a cake that day and all I needed to do was destroy the evidence. I hid the box under the mattress and plotted how to get rid of the cake. This presented a problem. The garbage can was not an option; he might see it there. So, I impulsively threw it out the window of our third story apartment, pondering the wisdom of throwing away a perfectly good piece of cake as I watched it tumble into the shrubbery below. Feeling better, I waited for Sam to come home. His first words upon arrival were something to the effect that there was a piece of cake in the bushes downstairs. I agreed that that was strange and went to boil water for the macaroni and cheese.

In the summer of 1974, Sam and I returned to the US and picked up our educational pursuits once again, both as juniors at Mississippi State University. We were much better students this time around, keeping busy with school and work-study jobs. I was hired at the Mississippi State Boll Weevil Lab, a sexy operation that researched the effect of sterilizing male boll weevils to mitigate infestations in cotton. Each day I counted the number of boll weevil eggs in plugs left behind by females, recording them carefully for posterity. It was almost as marketable a skill as making seat belt buzzers in Germany. Sam worked at the Soil Science Lab a few buildings over. We both graduated with honors two years later and moved back to Big Tom's farm near Merigold, where we would soon establish the first winery in Mississippi since Prohibition.

CHAPTER 9

Life in the Country

April 9, 1978
Commercial Appeal
Memphis, Tennessee
Delta Produces Its First Bottled Joy Since Prohibition
By William Thomas

. . . *"The trouble with having family do it," Rushing says, "is that you don't want to tell them not to sample the wine as they go along. It's the same thing when you have friends in to help you. By the end of the day, you get to thinking that maybe you ought to drive your friends home.*

All three of the Rushings—son, father and grandfather—joke about the unique problems of learning to work in the winery without consuming too much of the product.

"Every now and then one of the fermentation tanks in the basement springs a leak," Sam says, "but Granddaddy Tom won't tell me about it. He just puts a cup under the leak and the only way we know what's happened is when we see him making all these trips up the stairs with the cup."

The elder O.W. Rushing says the story is not quite accurate.

"The truth is," he said, grinning, "I watched that leak for about two days and then I told Sam about it. I said, 'You got to do something about that leak because it's getting the best of me.'"

The sheriff peered into the stairwell leading to the wine cellar, then began to make his way down into the cavernous space that, just the day before, had housed over eight thousand gallons of wine. Now the only remains were circling the drain and running down the hill on the other side of the east wall. A few minutes later, the sheriff climbed back up the stairs and eased down into an old rocker that sat near the wood-burning stove. He took out his notebook and settled in to ask a question or two.

"This Big Tom's chair?" he asked. I nodded in affirmation.

Big Tom, whose real name was Ottis Washington Rushing, was Sam's grandfather and an integral part of the operations at the winery. Born in 1898, his primary responsibility was to charm the britches off the endless stream of customers, mostly well-dressed ladies, who came through the place; he was very successful in this mission. To know Big Tom was to love him. Extremely handsome, even in his eighties, he had an uncanny gift of being able to intuit someone's place in space and meet him or her precisely there. He could banter with anyone from any walk of life, and not surprisingly, given his own history.

Big Tom was born the eighth of fifteen children to a poor farmer and his half-Choctaw wife in south Mississippi, near Tylertown. When the devastating cotton boll weevil hit the area around 1912, his parents loaded up the eight youngest children into their mule-pulled wagon and headed north to the Delta, where the timber was being cut and cleared to make way for the immensely profitable cotton crops to come. Those were desperate times in the Delta. There was no levee system running parallel to the Mississippi River back then, so extreme flooding most springs was a way of life. Houses were often built on stilts to accommodate the rising tides of the river. But sometimes even those weren't adequate, and the Delta pioneers spent week after week in the rafters, alongside their families and livestock. Cottonmouth snakes, black panthers, and huge mosquitoes further hampered the efforts of aspiring farmers such as Sam's great-grandfather, Sambo Rushing, poor as the dirt they had tried to farm two hundred miles south.

Big Tom had some incredible stories about these times, including the year he had to wear two left shoes because the commissary at Sunflower Plantation refused to return them to the factory. He had wonderful times to recount too, of course, but most were depressing. A particularly shocking one I recall was his telling me about the not-so-uncommon practice of simply murdering "the help" when the crops were harvested and pay day had come. These atrocities were usually staged as accidents, but not always. Often these young men had no family, and any effort toward pretense was just a waste of time. I have no way of verifying the accuracy of these claims, but he was not the only old-timer in the Delta to speak of this unthinkable practice.

Despite his hard upbringing, or perhaps because of it, Big Tom became quite a force as he grew into manhood. After serving a brief stint in France with the US Navy just as the Great War was coming to a close, he returned to the Delta and secured a job emptying the nickels out of the juke boxes in the area. Naturally this enterprise required a good deal of traveling the backroads from juke joint to juke joint, where he often ran into young Black blues singers. One in particular, Charley Patton, became a good friend, or as good a friend as he could be, given the times. Patton was an extremely talented musician who, only seven years older than Big Tom, had already established a prominent place in the world of blues music. He drew from his life experience, as did all blues players, and he had plenty to draw from. Married eight times, his throat slit once, Patton was reputed to have a bad temper. "But my goodness," recalled Big Tom, "could he make that guitar sing."

During the late 1920s, Big Tom was a deputy sheriff for Sunflower County. One night Charley Patton got into some trouble, and not the Good Trouble that John Lewis famously advocated. He had gotten tangled up in something at a local honky tonk and Big Tom felt compelled to arrest him, not for the first time. While sitting in his cell overnight, Patton wrote a song called "The Tom Rushen [*sic*] Blues," which he later recorded when he moved up North. Despite their friendship, he knew when he had crossed the line.

When you get in trouble, it's no use to screamin' and cryin',
Tom Rushen will take you, back to the prison house flyin'

Patton went on to become one of the most important blues musicians of his era. Many fascinating books have been written about him. It is not exactly a tribute to the times that his sad, tumultuous life story was not uncommon; as Big Tom often said, "They don't call it the blues for nothin.'" But Patton and his musical contemporaries provide important context for understanding the mystique of the Mississippi Delta.

Our venture into the wine business would have been impossible without Big Tom, for several reasons. First, it was to his farm that Sam and I moved upon graduating from Mississippi State in 1976. There was a small, run-down tenant house on the place that he let us renovate to live in. Situated on the site where the tea room would eventually be located, it sat on a knoll overlooking the Sunflower River. It was heaven to Sam and me, despite its rundown condition, covered with "roll on bricks" (asphalt siding made to look like bricks). I put my parents to work painting the inside of the place while I patched holes where mice and the occasional small squirrel liked to poke their heads through and make the scene. Mama generously donated her entire cache of Green Stamp books to the cause, about ten years' worth, enabling us to round out our household needs nicely.

My grandmother had died earlier that year, so Sam and I came into an antique furniture windfall just before graduating from State that spring. Some of the pieces had been in our family since pre–Civil War days and were quite beautiful. Others, well . . . not so much, but we were grateful for anything. Sam had picked up a used Ford Pinto cheap, unaware that particular model would later become famous for its gas tank exploding on impact. That, and our own little place on the farm, enabled us to begin our journey in adulting.

Adjacent to our palatial home sat Big Tom's garden. Situated on about half an acre, it featured row after row of beautiful green beans, tomatoes, onions, new potatoes, butter beans, peanuts, and squash. In the fall, he shoveled it all up and planted spinach, kale, and turnip greens. I am sorry to say I wasn't any help to Big Tom in this endeavor. While I enjoyed the vegetables, I explained to him, I never had been much of an outdoors person, especially when it was hot.

Sam's cousin, Felder Rushing, now a world-traveled garden journalist, was at the house one afternoon that first fall, 1976. His grandfather was one of Big Tom's fourteen siblings. He and Sam had just gotten back from boating up the Sunflower to check on some trot lines, where they snagged a sizable catfish which was now nailed to a post on our front porch for skinning. After showing Felder around the rest of the place, we came back to the house. The three of us sat on the front porch watching the river, sipping bourbon and Cokes, and eating boiled peanuts. Looking across our yard, Felder suddenly pointed out that I was obviously a planter, not a gardener.

"What's the difference?" I asked him, baffled by the distinction.

"Well, Di," he said, throwing a peanut shell over his shoulder, "just look at your flower bed." He placed another peanut between his pearly whites and cracked it open, looking at me through his blue-tinted, wire-framed glasses.

I studied the crosstie-bordered patch of emaciated flowers where zinnias, marigolds, and periwinkle seemed to be taking their last gasps. They did look pretty bad, now that I thought about it. I had spent a lot of time and a little money in May trying to establish what I was sure would be a paradisiacal retreat just off the porch. Sustainability has never been my strong suit, however, and as the Delta days became warmer, my zeal for a beautiful yard grew cooler. Now I found myself sitting on the porch steps with a garden expert surveying the sad remains of my ephemeral dream.

"What about it?" I could tell by my tone of voice that I was becoming a little defensive.

Felder choked on his drink, laughing. "Damn, Di, they're dead!" he said. "How often do you water them? Do you ever fertilize them? Mulch them?"

I didn't know what mulch was, but I wasn't about to tell him that. "Sure, I water them," I said. ". . . sometimes."

"That's what makes you a planter, not a gardener," Felder concluded. "Like a lot of folks you get caught up in spring, and all that. Then you go out and spend a fortune on flowers. A few weeks later, you forget about 'em." I realized he considered the whole enterprise a tragedy of sorts, so I changed the subject to football. I knew a lot more about that.

Our cocker spaniel, Ansbach, was as big a fan of the garden as anyone. Most summer mornings found him strolling down the row of tomatoes and judiciously selecting a plump juicy one. Pulling it off with his teeth, he would then lie down in the dirt and, holding it with his two paws, eat the whole thing. On the other side of the large garden was a tiny one-room shack where Big Tom would take his nap every afternoon after hoeing the rows of vegetables. He and his wife of sixty years lived about twelve miles away in Cleveland, so this was his second home. Each morning, Memaw packed his old tin lunchbox with canned sardines, crackers, an apple, and a few Fig Newtons. He and I sometimes sat in the swing on the front porch of our house and ate lunch together, watching the Sunflower River make its way to the Yazoo, south of us, and then finally to the Mighty Mississippi. Big Tom pointed out one day that Sam and I could put a boat in, right down the hill from our house, and drift all the way down to the French Quarters in New Orleans. I found the notion immensely appealing.

While violent crime was not an issue in those days, there was a bit of common ole thievery on our road from time to time. To discourage this, Big Tom fashioned a formidable looking cable that ran from under his cabin into the door sill. Neither end of the wire, however, was attached to anything, a fact indiscernible to anyone who might be tempted to trespass. I had to admit, it looked mighty intimidating, and I guess it worked, because in the twenty years he had his little cabin, it was never breached. Some sorry son of a bitch did, however, cut the top off the towering cedar in front of his cabin for a Christmas tree one year. I think that was the maddest I ever saw him.

Big Tom's next contribution to the effort was helping us round up the right folks to help us in this major experiment. Having grown up there, he knew most of the families in the area. Before long, we had a vineyard crew installing grape trellises and planting three varieties of muscadines—Carlos, Magnolia, and Noble. Big Tom and I got to work revamping the interior of the old dairy barn that stood next to our house. As we worked on the inside of the building, Sam began excavating the mound adjacent to the building to accommodate a huge cellar where six 3,000-gallon stainless steel tanks would go. A month later, they were lifted down by a crane from the top, and the roof of the cellar quickly followed. Over the course of the next few months, bottling equipment was ordered, followed by pallets of wine bottles from the Midwest. A bright red wine corker from Germany arrived and I immediately designed the flow of the assembly line around it. The "expertise" I had gained from the Bosch factory in Ansbach was finally paying off.

To tide us over until our own vineyards produced enough, we shipped in huge crates of grapes from a vineyard in north Arkansas. Day and night, we crushed them, ran them through the press, and sent the juice to the cellar to do its natural thing. When some of the wine was finally ready the next spring, we hired a few college kids from Delta State for the bottling line. They quickly found their groove, rock 'n' roll music competing with the clank, clank of the bottles as they worked. After a week or two, Sam discovered that the faster the music, the more productive the workers, so the Rolling Stones soon usurped the mellow rhythms of Pink Floyd and the Moody Blues.

A few years after the operation was up and running, Big Tom, then in his early eighties, became the undisputed superstar of the winery. Countless newspaper articles and television segments featured him for his colorful past and remarkable stories of the Delta. They wrote about his busting bootleggers in the swamps and his

singular connection to blues musicians. They described his role as
bartender extraordinaire at the Winery Rushing. On a more serious note, they also reported his incredible experiences as Bolivar
County Deputy Sheriff during the Great Flood of 1927, when the
Mississippi River inundated the Delta, taking the lives of over five
hundred people and leaving countless more homeless.

As journalists hastily took notes, Big Tom recounted tales of how
he helped the desperate folks who had been driven to the only high
ground, the levees that had been erected along the river, when it
overflowed. As the water crept farther and farther inland, Big Tom
took his rowboat to rescue sharecroppers, most of them Black, from
the roofs of their houses and deliver them to the top of the levee to
relief camps. Because the Delta bootleggers had the fastest boats, Big
Tom knew exactly where to go for help. Without exception, he told
the reporters, these "bayou riffraff" immediately stepped up to the
job, risking their lives as they rescued hundreds of residents from
their flooded homes. He helped them erect tent shelters and secure
provisions for their large families.

Despite the efforts of many, the living conditions were appalling.
Livestock, some alive and some dead, floated past the levee-dwellers
for weeks. Whole houses tumbled by, sometimes with people hanging on for dear life. Human remains were taken from the river and
pulled up to the levee banks. The stench, by all accounts, was unbear-
able, as people were trapped on the levee, week after week. Even
here, however, the caste system soon reared its ugly head. Some
were well-fed as others starved. At its peak, over seven hundred
thousand residents in multiple states along the lower Mississippi
were displaced by the Flood of 1927. Big Tom and the Bolivar County
Sheriff's Department were charged with the safekeeping of over
thirteen thousand of them.

By May of that year, the Mississippi River had grown to a width
of eighty miles. Big Tom told of how, when the water began to
recede months later, revealing the devastation to livestock, crops,
and homes, many of the sharecroppers talked of emigrating North

where opportunities seemed more promising. In response, he and other officers in local law enforcement were given strict orders to hold the sharecroppers captive on the levee for months, sometimes at gunpoint. While he never raised his shotgun, his face became solemn as he told me that others did. The wealthy planters of the Delta were terrified that if these laborers went North, there would be no one left to work the fields once things returned to normal. With their exit, they calculated, so would go their livelihood. The plan worked to a degree, but the Great Migration had already begun. The dreams of some were realized while the dreams of others died.

Two years later, Big Tom's friend Charley Patton composed and recorded a blues song entitled "High Water Everywhere," which told of the fate of these sharecroppers as they waited for the floodwaters to recede in the spring and summer of 1927. In the song, he claims, "I would go to the hill country, but they got me barred." I never asked Big Tom if he ran into Patton on the levee that year, but chances are good that he did. By 1929, Patton had moved up north, where he secured a contract with Paramount. "High Water Everywhere" soon came to be regarded as his magnum opus, and in 2001, Bob Dylan composed his own tribute to this masterpiece with his song entitled "High Water (for Charley Patton)."

In addition to the formidable task of patrolling the levee, Big Tom was assigned the duty of watching for "levee busters" that had taken up a nasty new occupation. He scouted the area each night for those attempting to row over to the Arkansas side of the river, boats loaded with dynamite. Desperate men from both sides were caught trying to blow up the levee on the opposite side of the Mississippi, directing the floodwaters away from their land by blasting away the earth barriers that protected those just across the river. He caught a few of these men and was proud of his work in this important endeavor. But, he said, that was just a small piece of the tragedy brought on by the Great Flood of 1927.

CHAPTER 10

Creating Our Own Reality

December 14, 1990
Clarksdale Press Register
Clarksdale, Mississippi
Merigold (AP)

*. . . Rushing, 38, said the winery was crippled by the loss of 8,000 gal-
lons, valued at about $160,000, that was dumped into the Sunflower
River during a May 3 break-in. The winery was not insured,
Rushing said.*

*Fired employee Emmit Ray Russell, 27, of Merigold was charged
with breaking into the winery May 3, opening Rushing's wine vats
and taking $401 in cash.*

As the Bolivar County Sheriff sat in the tasting room with Sam
and me, pondering the evidence of revenge that had been served
lukewarm, he continued to question us about who was most likely
to have done this. He repeated that it seemed "personal" and not
some random act of vandalism. As his rather insightful questioning
continued, Sam and I slowly came to realize that yes, there was one
person whose name naturally rose to the top: Ray Russell.

We explained to the sheriff that over a month before, in late
March, we had been forced to let one of our employees go after

learning of his illegal drug use. We didn't relate many details other than that, stating it was nothing we could prove. We added that upon his termination, Ray had been angry. We told the sheriff while we couldn't be sure he was responsible for what had happened, he seemed the most likely suspect. He knew of the family across the river and said he would investigate that angle. As he took meticulous notes, Sam and I looked at each other, dreading what was to come.

Ray was a good ole boy (read: white) who had grown up just across the Sunflower River from our farm. A couple of years earlier, his father had approached Sam to ask him to "give my boy a job." We didn't know much about the young man, then in his midtwenties, but we always needed help, especially in the vineyard. He came in, completed what passed for an interview, and began pruning vines that morning. Ray, along with several young students from nearby Delta State whom we hired each year, worked under the direction of our capable vineyard manager, Jack.

Ray worked across the bayou until the winter months arrived and Jack no longer needed extra help. As the college boys went back to class in the fall, Ray transitioned to the winery, where we crushed the grapes, ran them through the press, and pumped them into large stainless-steel tanks. From there, Sam ran tests and finessed the process as the wine fermented and aged. Ray never helped with the winemaking process, but he did assist in bottling, as well as tending bar when Big Tom was napping in his cabin or was down at the house, playing with the kids.

Ray lived with his parents, who farmed a patch of land just across the river. His father, Emmitt, was a short, stout man with a foul mouth, a defiant swagger and a growth of facial hair that didn't become fashionable until decades later. I never met his mother, but she seemed unimportant to either of the men in the family, except in terms of what she should be doing for them—fixing their meals, washing their clothes. Ray was rail thin, with light brown hair that matched his light brown teeth; he told me once he had started chewing tobacco when he was eight years old. Personable, he got on well with the people who came through the place and gave good tours of the winery to those who requested it. He worked cheerfully on the bottling line when needed, kept the tasting room tidy and the merchandise stocked. He was polite to everyone and seemed to fit in well. He appeared to take pride in his position at the winery and for a while there, we were happy to have hired him.

Unfortunately, as the business grew and the seasons changed, so did Ray. We began to see inklings of discontent, glimpses of resentment that were occasionally reflected in disturbing comments, sometimes about our dogs. Like all country places in the Delta, we had a collection of dogs that came and went through the years, some strays, some given to us. We became quite attached to all of them on varying levels. But Ray kept his distance from them, speaking harshly to them at times, when he didn't realize we were within hearing distance. I wasn't too concerned, however, as each evening they trotted happily behind my car to the house as I called it a day, returning home with us.

One afternoon a few months before the break-in, I was in the wine lab, which doubled as a storage area for the tea room. The ladies in the kitchen had gone home for the day and I was doing inventory for the weekly food order. Ray was around the corner in the tasting room, stocking the bar. I heard the front door of the winery open and close.

"Hey, boy," It was Emmitt, Ray's father. "What're you up to?" I resolved to stay put and be quiet. I was tired and not in the mood to make casual conversation with Ray's vulgar, leering father.

"Not much. What're you doin' here?"

"Oh, I had to go pick up that part for the tractor. That asshole at the John Deere place charged me over $300 for the part. Sorry sumbitch," Emmitt muttered. "You by yourself?"

"Yep," Ray said. Obviously, he was unaware of my presence in the next room. "Where's Sam?" Emmitt asked.

"Who the hell knows?" Ray responded. "Wherever he feels like goin', I reckon. Doin'," Ray added, "whatever he fucking . . . feels like

. . . doin.'" His voice was dripping with contempt as he slammed the wine cooler door shut.

"Well, ain't that real special," Emmitt sneered.

"Yep," Ray replied. Just dripping with it.

There was a pause. "I just came by to tell you Mama said we're eatin' early tonight. She gotta go up to Sister's. Anyway, don't be late."

"I ain't gonna be late," Ray said. The door closed again, and I heard Emmitt's truck start up in the parking lot.

I stood perfectly still. Ray resumed unloading the case of wine, the clanking of the bottles breaking the heavy silence. Closing the door to the cabinet quietly, I tiptoed toward the back door of the lab that led to the tea room. I was terrified that Ray would round the corner at any second. I held the screen door and closed it gently. I passed through the tea room kitchen and the swinging door that led to the dining room and sat down at the nearest table. My heart was pounding as I pondered the bizarre conversation I had just overheard.

What the hell?

I knew that Sam and I were never destined to become close friends with Ray; ours was a business relationship, among other reasons. But I was astonished by the measure of undisguised malice I had heard in the exchange between him and his father, a continuation, no doubt, of many that had come before.

Did I hear them right?

Yes, I certainly did.

Were they really that hateful?

Yes, they were.

I contemplated circumstances that could have prompted such spiteful rhetoric. I tried to recall things Sam and I had said that may have been misconstrued, coming up with nothing. Even though Ray had been a bit moody of late, I had thought that our relationship was solid. We joked around, paid him well, and complimented his work. Longing for insight, I flipped the script, examining how I felt about Ray and his father. I recognized that while I didn't know much about Ray's personal life, it had seemed pretty bumpy. He and his father were always engaged in confrontation with neighboring farmers over some minor thing or other. They were, to their mind, perpetual victims of a society that seemed anathema to their lifestyle. I had gone to school with kids from similar environments, and I knew their lives hadn't been easy.

In the fourth grade, I became friends with a little girl named Lottie, who lived in a four-room sharecropper shack with her parents and six siblings. She was smart, but too shy to let anyone know it. She had beautiful platinum-blonde hair and large brown eyes. Lottie and I bonded over a busy ant pile we discovered together on the playground one day. After that, we spent every recess together, when she was there, that is. She was often absent from school, as were her siblings. Through our conversations, I gathered that Lottie's father valued education little and women, even less. She told me that he and her uncles worked in the cotton fields every day and partied every night. Their social circle seemed to be limited to family and a few members of the country church they attended, known for snake-handling during the Wednesday evening services.

One afternoon, Mama offered Lottie a ride home from school. She and I chatted away in the back seat as we drove the three-mile distance. As we pulled up to her house, however, Lottie suddenly became very quiet. I looked over at her, then followed her gaze out the window. Rusted cars sat in the yard, littered by dozens of discarded beer and whiskey bottles. A small, hastily constructed dog pen held thin, mangy dogs. Chickens ran loose, pecking in the dirt. Her front porch leaned dangerously, attempting to support a gigantic TV antenna. Bags of trash, shredded by varmints, sat by the road. No shrub or flower was to be found, and the only clue to the current year was her father's shiny, tricked-out truck parked in the yard. After a moment, Lottie turned and looked at me. I held her hand and smiled as my young heart broke for her. She politely thanked my mother for the ride and got out of the car.

I had driven by houses like Lottie's all my life—there were hundreds of them in the Delta. But I had never known or loved anyone who lived in them. Lottie and I remained close friends until the end of the school year, when she and her family moved away. Mattie Akin Elementary, she told me, had been her eighth school in four years. When she left, she had no idea where her family was going. "Somewhere in Alabama, I think," she said.

I knew that the Russells' compound across the river wasn't much of a departure from Lottie's; I had driven by their place a few times. In their case, however, it wasn't lack of income that drove the decrepitude, as their economic situation was much better than Lottie's. In Emmitt's case, it seemed more lack of interest. The Russells had arrived in the Delta at about the same time as the Rushings, decades earlier, and they had probably been equally destitute. But as fate would have it, their paths unfolded in very different ways. It's hard to say why this happens—probably has a little to do with luck, truth be told. We like to think we are captains of our own destinies, but I haven't found that to be true. I think the head trip laid on most of us early in life—that we can be anything we want if we just work hard enough—is problematic at best. Sometimes it sets us up for failure. I aspired to be a quarterback for Ole Miss when I was in grade school, but I don't think any amount of hard work would have gotten me there. Most of us end up as some iteration of our early environment—politically, socially, and economically.

Ray likely felt that he didn't have much of a chance for upward mobility in life, rendering him hopeless for the most part. Like the citizens of the Soviet Union before satellite TV, he probably didn't know what he was missing in his early years. Travel wasn't in the cards for young Ray, again not because of lack of money—they had their own house, cars, and a valuable piece of land—but because of lack of curiosity. So, like the citizens of the Soviet Union, when Ray began to see that there was a bigger, better world out there, hopelessness morphed into resentment—towards us, towards others, towards life in general. In both cases, collapse was inevitable; hopelessness never ends well. Ray's mindset may be understandable, but it was misguided nonetheless, and dangerous for all concerned.

Looking back, I see that Ray's resentment manifested not long after he transitioned from the vineyard to the winery during his first few months with us. That was when our dogs began to go missing, and a few things from the office, including the accounts ledger, disappeared. Or maybe it had started long before that, when as a teenager, Ray watched the winery grow and prosper over the years from his rundown farm on the other side of the Sunflower. Either way, he had choices as an adult, as we all do. I wish that I had possessed the grace to understand, the insight to guide him to make better ones. But that wasn't to be, I'm afraid.

Sam and I told the sheriff that Ray had become highly erratic at times and lethargic at others. We noticed this, but we weren't too concerned because really, what young man in his twenties wasn't somewhat weird in a mercurial sort of way? And, for the sake of convenience, one often sees in one's employee what one wants to see; Sam and I certainly turned a blind eye towards Ray. Frankly, it was just easier to overlook what should have been red flags in the fall of 1989 and the spring of '90 than it was to address them. In retrospect, it seems that others at the winery seemed to be picking up on the devolution of Ray more than we, but little was said of the matter. At any rate, we concluded, life went on, and he continued to work for us for just over two years in all, doing his part to help grow the winery.

After we presented this anemic theory as to who might be responsible for the break-in and why, the sheriff closed his notebook and stood up.

"I'll drive on over to the Russells' right now and see what I can find out," he said. "Hopefully I can get some answers."

By the end of the conversation, Sam and I were certain that Ray was responsible—Occam's Razor and all that—but we also knew we had air-brushed the depiction of his termination a bit. In truth, the confrontation had progressed into a furious diatribe on Ray's part in which he had made some nasty threats. We told ourselves that if he were wise, he would get over it and move on. It turns out we sorely underestimated Ray's affinity and talent for the long game.

To this day, I don't understand why we didn't tell the sheriff the rest of the story that morning after the break-in. I think part of it was because we were in shock and not thinking clearly. But I think most of it was because it was such a distasteful, sordid experience, one we just didn't have the stomach to articulate. It didn't matter much, though; the sheriff would be back just a few hours later, when the rest of the story would unfold.

Before he left for his short trek to Ray's compound, the sheriff paused at the cypress-paneled bar in the winery's tasting room. He looked up at the framed awards and ribbons tucked among the antlers and other hunting trophies Sam had accumulated over the years.

"I remember when y'all won those ribbons for what—the best wine in the world, or somethin' like that?" he said.

"Not quite," I said, smiling. "But we were mighty proud to get them, that's for sure."

"We all were," the sheriff said, rubbing his chin. He took one last look, put his hat back on his head, and headed out the door.

CHAPTER 11

And the Winner Is . . .

February 1, 1979
Chicago Sun-Times
Chicago, Illinois
Mississippi vintner finds awards are sweet
By Tom Madden (United Press International)

In early 1977, Sam Rushing of Merigold had 300 acres of land and a dream of becoming Mississippi's first vintner. Today, his wines are award winners.

Rushing, 26, owns the only winery in Mississippi, and he is the first person in the state to legally produce wine since Prohibition. He recently came away with two awards in competition in Lancaster, Pa.

"We didn't have a vineyard, a winery—just an idea, a dream that we could do it," Rushing said. "All we had was a banker who believed in us."

Rushing's "Sweet White," made from imported grapes because his own plantings had not yet matured, was judged best in category in the "Wineries Unlimited" competition in November and his "Rushing Red" won a bronze medal in the American Red Division. Some 30 states and several Canadian wineries were represented in the meeting, where 379 wines were judged. It was the first time he had entered his wines in competition.

. . . "I feel good about it. For about a year the only checks I saw had my signature at the bottom. Now I'm seeing my name at the top for a change," he laughed.

Back in the parking lot in front of the winery, watching the sheriff drive away, Sam and I looked out over the lovely stretch of land that lay between us and the vineyard across the bayou. Our new house sat at the left end of a fork in the gravel road that ran past the winery and tea room, a beautiful winding pathway overlooking the river and the tributary that fed it, Beaver Bayou. It continued past the driveway to the right, leading down a steep little hill, over the narrow, rail-less bridge, and back up to the vineyard. Beyond the thirty-acre vineyard lay another couple of hundred acres where Sam planted the traditional crop of soybeans and wheat.

The vineyard was spectacular, especially during the fall harvest. Sam had devised a very sophisticated way to harvest the grapes. Jack drove the tractor pulling the tarpaulin-lined trailer while the college kids beat the hell out of the wires holding up the vines. An auger mechanism then caught the grapes and transferred them into the bins. Unlike traditional grapes, muscadines easily let go of the stems when they are ripe, so there wasn't the tedious cutting required as in traditional table grapes. September was the best time of the year and people from the whole area often came to watch us crush the grapes on the back pad of the winery. After the harvest each year, we encouraged select folks from the area to come pick the remnants, free of charge. This wasn't entirely altruistic on our part; we were usually thanked with little jars of wonderful, homemade muscadine jellies and jams.

Cousins to the varieties of grapes that grew in our vineyard were commonly found in the Delta, especially in the wooded areas. In those days our family spent a lot of time at Merigold Hunting Club, where we had a small cabin. Comprised of about 20,000 acres and just fifty members, the club was located inside the levee of the Mississippi River and was situated about twenty-five miles away from home. Effused with wild muscadines and other berries, it was prime real estate for hunting and had been for a long time. The club was chartered in 1922, and the founders, mostly farmers from Merigold, imported white-tailed deer from Minnesota, as well as turkeys, Russian wild boars, and other game. For nearly thirty years, they withheld from hunting the fertile fields and forests that comprised Merigold Hunting Club as they repopulated the game that had been wiped out decades earlier by hunters unconstrained by wardens and official hunting seasons. So unprecedented was the vision of this handful of men that eventually the Mississippi Game and Fish Commission determined these policies to be the gold standard, eventually adopting most of them for the state. It was a privilege to be a member of this world-renowned hunting paradise. Sam adored the club and spent a lot of time roaming the woods during the various hunting seasons.

There was a significant social component to Merigold Hunting Club as well. Most of our friends were members with small children, and we young mothers often spent the weekends at the club watching the kids play in the woods or on the sand bar of the Mississippi River. Baking in the sun, we drank Bourbon and beer (sometimes a lot), laughed, and talked about life. Years later, these old friends and I sometimes laugh about how carefree we were about child-rearing, admitting to each other that if our own children behaved as we had, we would likely be filing for custody of our grandchildren.

During gun season, the rustic old clubhouse served three meals each day, all of them showcasing the kill of the day. Boys and girls of all ages hung out by the gutting rack and watched as brand-new pickup trucks pulled up and unloaded deer, boar, and turkeys. They dreamed of the day they could hunt too, a day not as far into the future as one might think. The air was ripe with the combined odors of blood, guts, and whiskey, and the atmosphere crackled with excitement as the hunters regaled their fascinating stories of the hunt.

My best memories of Merigold Hunting Club, however, are of putting Lizzie and Matt to bed in our little cabin, lying there with them until they went to sleep as we listened to Prairie Home Companion on the small transistor radio there. When that was over, Sam and I would turn the radio off and listen to the sounds of the woods that surrounded the place, a pleasing combination of birds, crickets, and whatever else might be passing by. We loved this time together in the woods but were always ready to pack up and go back to the real world of work when the time came.

And work it was. Once we got it into our heads that we wanted to convert our 350-acre farm into part vineyard, it didn't take long to realize that our varietal options were limited. With the help of the Enology Department at our alma mater, Mississippi State University, we quickly learned that our best bet was with *Vitis rotundifolia* rather than the traditional *Vitis vinifera*, prevalent in other wine-growing areas of the world. Native to the south, muscadines didn't have much of a reputation as a wine grape; in fact, its reputation was such that we had a bit of repair work to do. In the past, the muscadine had been used to make very sweet, very strong homemade wines whose primary purpose was to advance what we call "Southern comfort." After our stint in Germany, however, Sam and I wanted to focus on producing palatable table wines to be enjoyed with meals.

The path to producing a decent wine proved long and arduous. But as Winston Churchill once said, "Success is stumbling from failure to failure with no loss of enthusiasm," and what we lacked in experience and expertise, we more than made up with in enthusiasm. After a couple of years, we were encouraged to take some of our first wines to the Wineries Unlimited competition in Pennsylvania.

Looking back, I imagine Sam and I painted quite the quaint picture for some of the stuffy Back-East oenophiles who roamed the venue that week. There we were, two twenty-somethings from the Mississippi Delta, trying to compete with wineries who had been in business for decades. Oblivious to our strong Southern accents, we repeatedly described our young venture with an earnest gravity that I am sure most found both endearing and annoying. We had so much to learn and to be truthful, we knew that, but our passion was unshakable. And I believe to this day that the thunderous applause we received upon walking up to the stage to receive our two Awards for Excellence at the end of the conference was genuine. It remains today a most cherished memory of our early days in the wine industry. In the years following, we won an additional six national awards for our wines, but none were as sweet as those won that first time.

CHAPTER 12

Mississippi Delta Estate Bottled

"The Mississippi Delta begins in the lobby of the Peabody
Hotel in Memphis and ends on Catfish Row in Vicksburg."
—DAVID COHN

October 14, 1984
Atlanta Journal-Constitution
Atlanta, Georgia
Mississippi Delta on the vine
By Raad Cawthon

The Sunflower River makes a lazy brown crawl through the flat cotton fields that make up the heart of the Mississippi Delta.

Away to the south, across a landscape that seems lonesome and empty—the geographical equivalent of the mournful blues that was born here—a dark plume of burning cotton waste rises like a signal against the warm October sky.

Sam Rushing has brought something most unexpected from this place: good wine.

. . . Across the slough from where Sam is standing, you can see 25 acres of risk shimmering under the sun.

The risk is muscadines.

. . . Now, after a three-year fight, Rushing has persuaded the U.S. Bureau of Alcohol, Firearms and Tobacco to designate the Mississippi Delta as a viticulture region.

It is the only official viticulture, or wine-producing region in the Southeast and the second largest, at 6,000 square miles, in the country.

Around the time our firstborn came along in the early eighties, Sam began an earnest campaign to have the Mississippi Delta designated as an official viticultural, or wine-producing, area of the United States. This was a long, involved process that required a tenacity and sense of purpose that I sorely lacked at the time, being a new mother and all. Since it also required a great deal of bureaucratic finagling, I lost interest in record time.

First, Sam was required to submit a petition to the US Department of the Treasury, Bureau of Alcohol, Tobacco and Firearms. According to the Federal Register / Vol. 48, No. 248, the ATF received the petition "proposing an area in northwestern Mississippi (with minute segments in Tennessee and Louisiana), as a viticultural area to be known as the 'Mississippi Delta.' The proposed area is leaf-shaped and extends for a length of about 180 miles with a maximum width of about 85 miles." Sam's petition also included a description of the growing conditions favorable to grapes and a paragraph alluding to the fact that the State of Mississippi had "invested millions of dollars in Mississippi State University's Enology Laboratory, located at Stoneville in the heart of the Delta region. This expenditure is based upon belief that the region will someday become 'the grape producing area of the Southeast . . .'"

The process proved to be as tedious and time-consuming as I had anticipated. Over a period of three years, Sam was required to produce summaries, backgrounds, plats, petitions, descriptions, legal boundaries, maps, and geographical descriptions, just to name some. While continually meeting the demands of our ever-growing wine business, Sam remained diligent and optimistic in his pursuit of a viticultural designation for the Delta.

I, on the other hand, was growing a bit weary of the seeming perpetuity of the whole legal endeavor. During this time, we had opened Top of the Cellar Tea Room and two months after that we learned with delight that I was expecting again. Exhausted and all martyred up one night in the summer of '84, I told Sam that we needed to either get it done or give it up. Matt was a month old, Lizzie was two, and I was tired of talking about it. Like most new mothers, I was a force to be reckoned with and Sam quickly concurred. Together we decided it was time to do a little lobbying in our nation's capital.

One of our favorite customers, born and raised in Merigold, proved to be quite valuable in our quest for help. We had last seen him at our 1983 Wine and Crawfish Festival, which was held on the banks of the Sunflower River by the winery. Our dear friends and neighbors to the west of us had established a successful crawfish business on part of their land a few years earlier and we decided to join forces for this annual event. The festival drew over a thousand folks and was great fun, with events such as a crawfish eating contest, a wine drinking (from baby bottles) contest, and a grape-stomping contest, whose lucky winner won the coveted "Prettiest Purple Foot" trophy.

Music from Delta blues legends such as Eddie Cusic and the Delta's own rock stars, the Tangents, provided the backdrop. The event started at 3:00 in the afternoon and ended promptly at dark-thirty with a spectacular fireworks display over the winery and Sunflower River. We were quite strict about wrapping it up then because, as we all know, after the sun goes down, the devil comes out.

The event was well-organized but casual, so when Larry pulled up to the festival that year in the back seat of a large black car chauffeured by a mean-looking bodyguard, it created quite a stir. That is, it did until everyone saw who it was, and then they went back to their business of talking, drinking wine, and eating crawfish. Larry Speakes, who at that time was serving as President Reagan's Acting White House Press Secretary, folded into the crowd without missing a beat, shaking hands while balancing a glass of wine. He had always been a good customer of ours, visiting at least once a year when he came down to check on his elderly parents, life-long citizens of Merigold. Larry had stepped into his position suddenly on March 30, 1981, when an assassination attempt on Reagan resulted in his injury as well as that of Press Secretary James Brady. Larry then continued to serve in the Reagan administration for the next seven years. So, when it appeared that we were being stonewalled with our Appellation of Origin application in DC, Sam gave Larry a call.

Sam said the conversation with Larry lasted about ten minutes. Half an hour later, the US Secretary of the Treasury called him.

"Mr. Rushing, I understand you have a question for me," he began. Sam went on to outline the Cliffs Notes version of his petition and within a few days, it was approved by the Bureau of Alcohol, Tobacco and Firearms. We celebrated with a bottle of wine and sent a couple more up to DC as a thank you. A few weeks later, we received a warm personal letter from President Reagan, thanking us for the wine. While we weren't particularly fans of Reagan, we did feel like big shots for a little while.

On October 1, 1984, the Mississippi Delta was designated the first viticultural region in the Southeastern US, enabling us to label the wine's appellation of origin as "Mississippi Delta Estate Bottled." Of course, a ceremony was in order, so we soon held it on the grounds near the winery and tea room. Those in attendance included Mississippi State's head of the Enology Department, other MSU professors who had helped over the years, and the requisite Mississippi politicians, all of whom spoke highly of the momentous achievement. The ceremony concluded with the burial of a time capsule which was capped with a beautiful marble marker carved in the shape of Mississippi. The items in the capsule included the first bottle of Mississippi Delta Estate Bottled Wine, the letters supporting the application, that day's newspaper, Matt's baby shoe, a 1984-coin proof set, and numerous other things I can't recall.

Many years later, one of the Meyer boys from Merigold was coming to Ouray for a visit. Before he left, he offered to dig up the time capsule and bring it home to us in Colorado. Six feet deep, it was not an easy task to extricate it, and we appreciated the thoughtful offer. Since the farm changed hands long ago, we are glad to have it back. Today, it resides in our attic here in Ouray. I don't know if or when we will ever open it. We don't remember many of the things we had placed inside of it, and that's okay. It serves as a reminder that we don't need to know everything, all the time.

CHAPTER 13

Hearts Are Broken

May 1990
Crime Scene Search Evidence Report

Name of Subject: Emmitt Ray Russell
Offense: Burglary of Winery Rushing
Date of incident: 05-04-90 Time——AM–PM
Evidence Description: General Ledger Book
Property of Winery Rushing
Location: Defendant's Bedroom in Drawer of Chiferobe [sic]
(Personal note: This information was recorded on a sticker affixed
to the front cover of our ledger when it was returned to us later,
after the trial. The officer had found it in Ray's closet. I remember
it struck me then as disturbing—our old business records tucked
between Ray's personal garments.)

Just a few hours after he had left, we heard the sheriff pull back into the winery parking lot again. He and the Bolivar County Investigator entered the tasting room, each carrying black evidence bags. The electric energy emanating from the two men was palpable. The sheriff placed the contents onto the bar, and an old hammer wrapped in a clear bag slid out, followed by a pair of blue jeans, soaked in wine. The scent was overpowering.

"Found these on the floor of Ray's living room," the sheriff said, pushing the wine-stained evidence toward us. "This, too." He picked up the hammer in his gloved hand and we could see a few shards of glass still embedded in the wooden handle. I recognized it as the one Sam kept in the office.

"I reckon we got the right man, all right," the sheriff said. He told us that after talking with us that morning and learning of our confrontation with Ray six weeks before, he and his chief investigator found sufficient cause to call on him for questioning. For reasons unknown but certainly surmised, Ray did not have the presence of mind to conduct the conversation outside, and he invited them into his house. Evidence of his crime, we learned, was strewn everywhere. Most conspicuous, however, was the strong odor of wine that permeated the rooms.

Grabbing a smaller bag from the bar top, the sheriff asked, "This look familiar?" He pulled out a thick black ledger and placed it on the bar of the tasting room. Sam and I looked at it, astounded.

"What . . . where the hell did you find this?" Sam asked, picking up the four-inch-thick tome with dozens of pink invoices sticking out from the tops of the pages. The ledger had disappeared almost two years before, not long after Ray had started working in the winery. It held the names, addresses, and unpaid invoices of the hundreds of liquor stores with whom we were doing business at the time. While we had one of the first Apple computers that was made affordable in the early nineties, those were the days before electronic spread sheets were user friendly, and Sam was still using the old, time-proven accounting methods.

Sam told the sheriff that the ledger had gone missing nearly two years before, recalling the difficulty we had in trying to reconstruct its contents by looking at shipping records and calling our customers, all of whom were honest in their reckoning. After looking for the ledger for hours, we had concluded that it had somehow fallen into the trash can in the office and been inadvertently thrown away.

Never had we suspected something like this, nor did we ever figure out how or why he stole it.

"I found it in Ray's bedroom, along with these," the sheriff said. "Can you tell me anything about these?"

The sheriff was uncharacteristically somber as he reached into his pocket and laid several worn dog collars on the bar. Our hearts sank as we recognized the collars of our beloved dogs that had died or gone missing over the years. Two of them had names engraved on little gold hearts that dangled along with the vaccination tags. The newer, shinier one had recently adorned the neck of our dear Socks. Amid the tragedy of finding him, we hadn't even realized that it was missing. The other tag read, "Oreo Rushing." Lizzie and Matt had named the Australian Shepherd puppy that because he was black and white and very sweet.

One morning two years earlier, Lizzie had gone outside to play with Oreo. She found him dead on our front porch. She recalls to this day the dreadful details of his remains, all of which pointed to his having been poisoned. Of course, we wondered briefly if it had been intentional, but it seemed much more likely that he had gotten into some chemicals we had sitting around the place; everything from antifreeze to weedkillers sat in storage at various locations on the farm. Sam and I felt terrible that we had been negligent in securing these containers, but we were fairly sure that was the cause of Oreo's death. Now we knew. Looking at his worn blue collar, we finally learned what had happened to Oreo and two other pups who had gone missing over the last couple of years. For better or worse, we never learned the details of their demise at the hand of Ray.

Holding the dog collars in my hand, I looked at the sheriff as we told him the rest of the story we had begun that morning. We described in sad detail the events that had unfolded just over a month earlier, events that we had failed to report for various reasons, events that had undoubtedly culminated in that May morning's appalling discoveries.

I began by telling the sheriff that our family had returned home from the hunting club one morning about six weeks earlier to find our sweet little dog, Socks, lying just outside the doggie door on the front porch, looking up at us and weakly wagging his tail. He had been shot through the throat. We immediately scooped him up and rushed him to nearby Cleveland to the veterinarian, who agreed to meet us at the clinic. She told us that while the wound itself was not life-threatening, it remained to be seen whether he would be able to eat and therefore survive. We checked him in and the next day she performed surgery to try to reconstruct the muscles in his throat that enabled him to swallow. Despite valiant efforts by the vet and Socks, after three days we were forced to surrender the fight. He had tried to eat, the vet told us, but the food literally fell from the hole in his throat. Sam and I held him as he was put to sleep. I stroked his soft head as he took his last breath.

That was heartbreaking. What we found upon entering our home after returning from the vet that night, however, was ominously portentous. Passing the small pool of blood where Socks had lain just a few hours earlier, we entered the living room of our house to find sizable chunks of sheet rock strewn about the carpet. This part of our house featured vaulted ceilings, and as I studied the debris, I looked up to see its source. Above were three or four holes piercing the white ceiling, obviously caused by a high-powered rifle. Whoever had shot our little dog had also shot up our home.

Anyone who has had something like this happen will be the first to tell you that he or she is never quite the same again. It doesn't matter if the offender is caught or not; a piece of trust is irrevocably lost. The more someone is victimized, the stronger the wariness grows, despite brave and conscious efforts to stem its pernicious hold. This was the Rushing family's first inkling of a world that we had never intersected before, and I felt the ugliness it represented deep within my core. I was terrified. I didn't know if someone was still in the house, or if someone had touched my daughter's blanket, or my son's

Garfield stuffy. Everything in the house felt contaminated, and it was a long time before that feeling passed.

Sam told us to go back outside, away from the house. Lizzie, Matt, and I stood behind the truck, listening to the crickets harmonize in the evening's quietude. We watched in silence as the lights in our home came on room by room, tracing Sam's steps as he searched, unarmed, for an intruder. The minutes that passed by seemed interminable. The singing of the crickets abruptly ceased when he finally stepped back onto the porch.

"Everything seems to be okay," Sam said, looking at me with an expression that belied his words.

That night, we called around to see if anyone had noticed anything unusual the night before. One neighbor down the road said he had seen an old green Mercury pull into the winery parking lot around eleven o'clock. He went on to tell us that he hadn't thought much about it when he saw it, though, because he was pretty sure it was the one "that Russell boy" drove, and he knew he worked for us.

The next day, Sam and I drove into Merigold to talk with a few "reliable" citizens about what we had found the night before. A couple of them kicked at the dirt as they admitted hearing some rumors about Ray's reputation with drugs. One, it turned out, offered a bit more insight. Despite his personal choices, we still considered him a friend of sorts. It was, after all, a small town.

"Well," he said, scratching his head as we stood in his driveway, his hunting dogs circling our legs, "I don't rightly know, but seems I heard some things about Ray dealin' drugs late at night out at your place. But I didn't want to say nothing because you know how people talk and everything . . . I wasn't sure."

"Yeah, well, someone shot our dog while we were gone Saturday night," I told him. "And they shot up our house. We need to find out who it was."

"Mighta been Ray," the man reluctantly admitted. "Seems like I heard he was out there Saturday night. That's where he told a friend of mine to meet him, out there in your parking lot." He leaned over to scratch the silky ears of one of the hound dogs, pondering, no doubt, the wisdom of his revelation.

Sam and I looked at each other. I don't know which aspect of this conversation we found more astonishing, this man's cluelessness or, more importantly, our own.

"And how long has this been going on?" Sam finally asked.

"Oh you know . . . a while I guess." He stood up and finally looked us directly in the eye. "You know how them Russells are. I didn't want to start nothin'. Still don't." We understood why he was hesitant to get involved, especially given the reputation of Ray and his father in those parts. I am not sure I would have said anything either; I wasn't particularly courageous back then.

As Sam and I talked later that morning, pieces of the puzzle fell into place—the mood swings, his listlessness followed by volatile behavior, the gnashing of his teeth as he talked. Somewhat of an innocent in this regard, I hadn't recognized the hallmarks of drug use, but we were slowly coming to terms with the reality of Ray's role in what had conspired at our house the night before. I think that was when we finally admitted to each other the subtle shift we had both noticed in Ray's demeanor. Each day he had become less engaged, more resentful, eager to get the customers in and out quickly. He was losing weight and had begun grinding his teeth incessantly. But the reality was that we had ignored these signs because, simply put, it was easier to do that than to confront him and deal with the contentious fallout that would inevitably follow. The prospect of firing him was so unappealing that Sam and I never once discussed Ray's seeming decline.

I can't speak for Sam, but in retrospect, I think that subconsciously I have always felt that by expressing something out loud, something fear-driven, I am giving it permission to come right in my front door and have a seat at the kitchen table. I was afraid that somehow, in talking to someone about Ray's sporadic behavior, the threat would become even more imminent. In due time, I would realize the absurdity of that belief. Circumstances that followed that year schooled me well how to perceive, predict, and thus prevent. They taught me to listen attentively to intuition, that the tiniest niggling in my heart is there for a good reason and invariably in my best interest. The lessons I learned that year remain among my most valuable life tools.

Unfortunately, by then, Ray had begun to feel that he was an essential part of the winery, indispensable. Instead of recognizing the potential hazards of that mindset, we appreciated it, dangerously mistaking what he felt as entitlement for some curious brand of loyalty. But as we all know, familiarity breeds contempt, and this time-honored maxim best explains the events that followed. Later that day, after talking to a few more sources—in a small town, everyone knows who they are—we were able to confirm that Ray had indeed become involved in a nefarious, albeit small-time, drug trafficking trade. We also learned that the parking lot of the winery had become the late-night rendezvous point for many of these deals, a place about two football fields away from where our young family slept each night, oblivious to the crimes being committed just down the dirt lane.

As Sam and I debated the best way to handle Ray, who was due in for work the next morning, I kept insisting that we just "let him go and move on with our lives." I was fearful of retribution from Ray and his father, should we report him to the sheriff. I remember Lizzie appeared at the kitchen door several times that night as this conversation ensued, upset by Socks, the looks on her parents' faces, and the sudden collapse of the safety of her home.

"What's the matter, Mama?" Her blue eyes were huge behind her pink glasses as she stood in the doorway in her Strawberry Shortcake nightie, trying to understand why her life had taken such a sudden, dark turn. We scooted her back to bed, unable to answer her question. Against his better instincts, Sam finally agreed to just let Ray go without reporting it to the authorities. We spent a sleepless night dreading the conversation to come the next morning.

Of course, it fell to Sam to confront Ray as he unlocked the
entrance to the winery and entered the tasting room the next morning, unaware that we had pieced together the events of the weekend
before. I was listening from the adjacent office, door closed, as Ray
entered the tasting room and mumbled, "Mornin." In the late hours of
the night before, Sam and I had decided he would begin by questioning Ray about his whereabouts on Friday night. We knew by then that
he had met someone in the parking lot that night and we knew why.

At first, he denied being there at all, but as Sam calmly related the
details he had unearthed, Ray finally admitted to being there late
that night, claiming he had come back to "check on whether he had
locked the door." Even he knew how ridiculous an assertion this was,
as he was never the last to leave the winery for the day. Sam continued to question him about the events, finally getting to the crux of
the matter: We knew that Ray had been dealing drugs in the winery
parking lot. Sam concluded by stating that we also suspected that he
had shot our dog and the roof of our house the previous weekend.
When Sam made it clear that he would no longer be working for
us, Ray exploded.

"You can't fire me!" he said over and over, a litany so bizarre that
I can vividly hear it in my mind even now, decades later. Finally,
after pleading, then threatening, he understood that it was over and
stormed out the door, got in his dusty green Mercury, and sped away.

As we told the sheriff that afternoon, we fervently wished we had
done the brave thing and called his department after finding our
little dog and our bullet-ridden house that evening. But the reality
was that it was all hearsay, and even we knew that was not enough
to make any charges stick. We also considered that we couldn't go
forward with any accusations without involving friends and what
they had learned, and we knew that would not end well for them.
Further complicating the matter was the fact that Ray and his gun-
toting father lived right across the river. As I sat there holding Socks's
collar in my hand, I knew that we had been right about Ray, a con-
firmation that was more disturbing than it was vindicating.

We concluded by telling the sheriff that in the weeks following, things seemed to settle down, until that morning, of course. Sam said that after finding Socks, we were shaken but resolved to carry on. I confessed that for me, that was a tenuous effort at best. There were times I was convinced that surely Ray had realized that he had dodged a bullet since we had decided not to report him. Other times, I said, I was certain that this was just the beginning.

After we finished our story, the sheriff looked at us and took a deep breath. "Well, it's over now," he said. "We have Ray Russell in custody."

CHAPTER 14

And Just How High Is That?

July 8, 1990
Commercial Appeal
Memphis, Tennessee
The Delta remains home to the mythical South
By Rheta Grimsley Johnson

When non-Southerners think of the South, the Delta is what they imagine. It is the South of fiction and fantasy, of forever fields and proper ladies and slow-motion nights. This is the only place left in America with bona fide shacks and mansions side by side, with not enough middle class to blunt the dramatic disparity. The black soil here rivals that of the Valley Nile, and mosquitoes come big as hawks.

. . . Each time I come here I am smitten all over again. It's not the stark beauty, as evident and real at the lonely Parchman prison farm as at the finest house, or the writers and artists who colonize here, or even the stubborn gentility that lays a gloved hand across all conversational exchange, even when someone hates your guts.

. . . Things are still slow and civilized here. People speak in an unhurried, florid way and bring one another gossip and vegetables from the lush landscape.

. . . I rode with a friend out Cleveland's Bayou Road, past crape myrtle trees the red of rooster wattles, through humidity you could slice, toward Merigold, where the McCartys make their celebrated

pottery and eat popcorn with a spoon, and where Mississippi's first winery since Prohibition, Winery Rushing, is located.

Tragedy had befallen the winery recently when a disgruntled former employee ransacked the restaurant and poured much of the muscadine wine inventory into the Sunflower River.

At once the faithful patrons came, bringing covered dishes and offers of help. Someone said it resembled the attentions usually reserved for a death. The winery is not just a successful family-owned business; it is a pleasant oddity, something distinctive and full of ambience the Delta craves. People want to do it well.

The sheriff collected the ledger, the reeking blue jeans, and the dog tags and put them back into the evidence bags. As we stood there wrapping up the interview at the bar, I became more and more cognizant of how irresponsible, if not delusional, we had been to try to handle the crisis on our own the previous month. We had acted in good faith, to be sure, and we knew we couldn't prove anything that had happened in those final days of March. But I felt chastened, nonetheless.

On his way out, the sheriff told us that a large sum of cash had also been found in Ray's bedroom, and that he would be held indefinitely on bail. He tried to reassure us that they would do all they could to see that justice was served. We knew they were sincere, and the remarks were kind, but they did not resonate with either Sam or me.

As Sam walked the sheriff and investigator to the parking lot, I went back into the office to begin processing all that had occurred that day. A few minutes later, Sam came in, his face ashen.

"What . . . what's the matter, Sam?"

"He's out there. . . . He's in the sheriff's car," he said.

"Who is?" I asked. I truly had no idea.

"Ray," he said. "He's in the backseat, handcuffed. He looked straight at me the whole time I was talking to the sheriff."

"Wait . . . what?"

"And while he was looking at me, he was smiling, Di. That sorry son of a bitch was sitting there, smiling." Sam sat down on a case of wine sitting by his desk. Elbows on his knees, he looked at the floor and ran his fingers through his hair. Then he looked back up at me.

"I don't think this is over, Di. I don't think he is finished with us."

And I knew Sam was right. I could envision Ray's wandering around their rundown compound just across the river from our house, his sense of rage growing in direct proportion to some irrational, perverse sense of victimization. I could easily picture his sitting around with his boorish father, getting high at their house, watching TV while plotting revenge with varying degrees of cruelty and efficiency. The conversation I had overheard between them at the winery played an endless loop in my head, *Well ain't that real special. . . .*

We never learned the exact sequence of the events that night at the winery but, as is often the case, the truth emerged later as we learned that Ray had taken the path of so many of his ilk. On the night of the break-in at the winery, before anyone knew about it, a clerk at Merigold's only convenience store had overheard him boasting about his exploits that evening. Dismissing it as false braggadocio at the time and paying little attention, the clerk called us a few days later to tell us what he had heard. He said that Ray had come in just before closing time that night to buy some beer. Standing in line, he had delivered a drunken, incoherent diatribe on how he had "brought them Rushings down a notch or two."

"That boy," the clerk concluded, "was high as a giraffe's toupee."

The next day, the TV and newspaper crews began arriving in droves. Of course, in 1990, Facebook was just a twinkle in Zuckerberg's eye. But even then, there were other means of swift communication, and it took only a few hours for word of the break-in to become public. Crews from all over the mid-South, Memphis, Jackson, and smaller towns in between, descended upon us, seemingly simultaneously.

I remember standing alone in the tea room kitchen that afternoon, trying to process where to begin, when a beautiful young reporter from Memphis walked in the back door, microphone in her hand, camera lights blaring behind her. I clearly recall her perfectly polished fingernails grasping the mic and her eighties-style big hair, thinking, "Who the hell does she think she is?" quickly followed by, "And how could she have possibly had the time to do her hair?" It's strange how, when tragedy strikes one personally, the world continues to turn, cruel in its disregard. My reaction was raw outrage.

I shouted at her, pointing towards the door, telling her, "Get the hell out of my tea room!" I then covered my face and began sobbing. To her credit, she acquiesced quickly, but her well-written and surprisingly accurate report did appear on Memphis television that night. I was grateful that my meltdown had remained on the cutting floor.

Sam and I sat in stunned silence that evening, watching station after station showing TV coverage of the shambles left behind by Ray. It was easy to discern those seasoned reporters who were familiar with our fourteen-year-old story from those who were new to the game; the variation in empathy was stunningly apparent. Unbeknownst to us at the time, several crews had quietly taken footage of the activity on the grounds that morning—footage of Shirley picking shards of glass out of the colorful window boxes under the tea room windows, tears running down her face. Footage of Roberta and Flo somberly sweeping up the remains of Ray's handiwork in the main dining room, and of Sam mopping the wine cellar, stoic and silent. Footage of Jack, standing outside the winery off to the side, slowly shaking his head and kicking the ground with his foot. Over a hundred neighbors and customers had lined the outskirts of the parking lot, hats in hand, lugubrious, as though attending the funeral of a close friend. Reporters were everywhere that day it seemed. And for the first time since opening the winery, I did not welcome the attention and its subsequent financial boost.

I didn't feel angry that night as I sat in front of the television, working on my fourth glass of wine and wondering how we would ever recover from our personal and financial loss. I tuned in as news anchors speculated on the cause of the break-in and what it would mean for the survival of the Winery Rushing and Top of the Cellar Tea Room. I listened as they reported that a disgruntled former employee had been arrested that afternoon, flashing Ray's mugshot on the small screen in my bedroom. With a heavy heart, I watched interview after interview of neighbors, customers, and law enforcement officers. But I didn't feel angry. Instead, for some reason I still don't understand, I felt deeply embarrassed and ashamed.

CHAPTER 15

Waiting for the Other Shoe

May 7, 1990
Bolivar Commercial
Cleveland, Mississippi
Burglar ransacks Merigold winery
By Robert H. Smith

The Sunflower River ran red Thursday night and Friday morning three miles east of Merigold, as 8,000 gallons of native Bolivar County wines were discharged into it during a burglary of the Winery Rushing.

The intruder opened a valve at the base of each vat, releasing the wine to escape through floor drains into the river below.

Sam Rushing, 38, who operates the winery in partnership with his father, estimated the value of lost wine at $150,000 to $200,000. Rushing added that he held no insurance on his product, making the loss irrevocable.

He was quick, however, to accentuate the positive, and to comment on the support he's received from friends and neighbors.

. . . Rushing and his wife, Diane, will be counting on the Winery Tea Room, a restaurant operated in conjunction with the winery, for income in the short run.

. . . Before Friday was out, the investigators arrested Emmitt Ray Russell, 27, of Merigold in connection with the incident, charging him with burglary of a commercial establishment.

Russell bonded out of the Bolivar County jail, paying the
required $2,000 of his $20,000 bond. . . . His case will be presented
to the May 21 grand jury.

Because Ray stole a few hundred dollars from the office that night, the crime that derailed our family was eventually classified as Burglary of a Commercial Establishment. There existed, we were told, no charge that could accurately reflect someone's disposing of nearly a quarter million dollars' worth of wine by letting it go down the drain. Fair enough, I guess; some things just can't be anticipated. Still, it seemed to us that this charge was grossly inadequate in capturing what had happened in fact. What about the loss of the wine, our livelihood? Vandalism? The murder of our precious dogs? When we asked the powers-that-be about this, we were assured over and over that the case would be a slam-dunk, and that Ray would "go to jail for a long time." This was hardly our area of expertise, so we accepted these assurances as truths as we attempted to rebuild our lives. It was easy to do; no one we knew, including the Sheriff's Department, thought for a moment that Ray would be vindicated.

A couple of weeks after Socks's death, a friend of ours who raised beautiful black Labrador Retrievers offered us a new puppy. We named her Sassy, short for Sassafras. Unlike her predecessors, Sassy went everywhere with us. With Ray out of the picture and the kids still inconsolable on the loss of Socks, we had decided it was time to try to recapture a little normalcy in our lives. Sassy was magnificent—sleek, shiny, and full of joy. She and Matt, then six, often played tackle football in our front yard. Much bigger than "the baby," Sassy played tackle to Matt's offense; typically, Sassy prevailed. Lizzie was, of course, the referee, and the three of them quickly became inseparable.

Also around that time we hired a delightful young man from Merigold to take over the tours and tastings. James was young and energetic and excited to be the newest addition to the Winery

Rushing. The customers immediately took to him as he poured samples of wine and fielded countless words of sympathy with style and grace. He took them to the cellar, now devoid of wine, and explained the process as though nothing had happened, describing in detail the new vintages and labels we had on the drawing board. We felt, correctly, that we had exercised better judgment this time around.

The days that followed were characterized by clean-up, paint, construction, and the occasional fifteen-minute break. Needed materials to get the tea room up and running again appeared at our doorstep on the third day, paid for by an anonymous donor. Friends and customers showed up to help. Sam and I avoided newspapers and TV coverage that week but learned later that the events of May 4 were recounted in exhaustive detail all over the mid-South. We took comfort in the support we were receiving and focused entirely on opening again.

Fortunately, Ray had not ventured into the warehouse during his midnight ransack, so we still had a few hundred cases bottled and packed for shipping. To get the most we could from those, we had to reserve them for on-site winery sales, which brought in retail dollars instead of wholesale. We contacted our accounts and told them that we would be unable to ship out for a while. They all knew the story by then and understood. Some generously offered to prepay for future orders, saying that they were confident we would be on our feet soon and that they were behind us all the way. It felt good.

About a week after the break-in, our insurance agent came by to tell us he would be "more 'n willin'" to testify that we would receive no payment as a result of the incident. We already knew that our policy did not cover burglary or vandalism. In hindsight, this was a generous offer on his part; not everyone is willing to get involved in matters of a criminal nature. We thanked him and told him that wouldn't be necessary. Because Support and Optimism like to hold hands, we felt that Ray would be convicted and that we would survive the ordeal. On May 10, Top of the Cellar reopened and was immediately booked solid for weeks in advance.

Matt and Lizzie were wrapping up their final days of kindergarten and second grade, and because ours was such a small community, all their classmates knew at least part of the story. At times they took comfort in the sympathy they received and even milked it a bit. More often, however, they resisted it; they just wanted their old lives back. Of course, they didn't understand the dance of the days' dynamics but in fairness, neither did anyone else.

Strong, resilient, unstoppable—those were the adjectives I chose to embrace in the daytime as I worked at the tea room and cared for my family. At night, though, I was painfully fragile. When we learned that Ray had posted bond the very next day after his arrest, I was stunned. How could that be? But there he was—sleeping in his own bed, eating at his own kitchen table, less than half a mile away. Night after night, I woke up to look out our bedroom window, searching for his old green car by the winery. Night after night, I tiptoed to the kids' rooms to make sure they were still there.

I doubt that it was coincidence that Lizzie and Matt had taken to sleeping together in Matt's bed after that. It broke my heart to see them snuggled close to each other for security. Sometimes, as I watched them sleep, I noticed their little fists were clenched, and I wondered how the recent events would affect their health, their lives, in the long term. I stood in my nightgown over their bed every night, listening to them breathe as the crickets' choir harmonized just outside the window. How, I asked myself, did we get to this place? What red flags had we missed? I was consumed by guilt, paralyzed by fear. In the darkness of Matt's room, I came to understand that while fear is not always followed by guilt, guilt is invariably accompanied by fear—fear that one didn't do everything possible to thwart the tragedy. I don't think it matters that sometimes averting the disaster is nigh impossible.

I was not the only night wanderer that summer. During those weeks, the kids often got up during the night and climbed into our bed. This, along with any little sound, woke me up with a jolt, and the wear and tear on my body soon became apparent. I lost weight and developed bags under my eyes that would have required my checking them in at the airport gate, had I the means to go anywhere. Within weeks, I was taking strong sleeping pills so that I could function during the day, a habit that continued for a long time and took a great deal of effort to break. They helped me sleep, but only for a few hours.

One night as I lay awake, I remembered my brother telling me about the provenance of the expression, "Waiting for the other shoe to drop." One version, his version at least, was that it originated in the New York City apartment buildings of the early twentieth century, specifically those that were not insulated for sound. The tenant below could easily hear when the person living above was ending his day. He took his shoes off, dropping them onto the floor beside the bed. After one dropped, another would inevitably follow.

That's how I felt each night as I stared at the ceiling, as though I had heard the first thump and was waiting for the next one. I explored the paradox that people like Ray often find it impossible to "forgive" someone that they, in fact, have wronged—something to do with justifying their own actions, I suppose. And I was certain that he was not finished with us.

That summer, I spent night after night, waking every thirty minutes or so to look out the window to see if anything was amiss. I would check the locks, check the kids, and then try like hell to check the paranoia. Waiting for the other shoe to drop was an excruciating exercise in futility. That is, it was for a little while.

CHAPTER 16

Just Tryin' to Pay the Bills, Ma'am

December 25, 1985
San Jose Mercury News
San Jose, California
Muffin mix's popularity spreads
By Malcolm Hebert

In the past 28 years of writing about food and wines, I have seen many ideas for promoting wine. The earliest was a wine toothpaste introduced in Chicago almost 25 years ago. It was quickly followed by a wine gum, a wine shaving cream and a wine breath freshener.

. . . Therefore I wasn't too surprised to learn about a new wine muffin mix. What did surprise me, however, was finding out that it is successful in the South. It is so successful, in fact, that the inventor and his wife are planning national distribution of the product by March.

Sam and Diane Rushing, owners and operators of The Rushing Winery and the Top of the Cellar Tea Room in Merigold, Miss., created Rushing Original Wine Muffin Mix.

. . . The mix is versatile: You can create 18 of your own muffins using any wine you like. If sweet muffins are your bag, try a cream sherry or sweet sauterne.

. . . In the past several weeks, I have used gewürztraminer and cream sherry in my two muffin tests and both turned out great. It isn't hard to get used to eating sherry wine muffins with ham and eggs.

It did not take long to run out of the bottled wine in the warehouse that had been spared that night. Once we reopened, demand for Rushing Wine and tea room reservations escalated exponentially. It seemed as though our customers sensed we had narrowly dodged a bullet, that bullet being the complete demise of the winery and tea room. Our grape harvest for the coming September looked promising, but the proceeds from that would not be realized for quite some time. Heavy research into nouveau wines began. Sam felt we could have a new 1990 wine available the following winter, if all went well, and he worked hard to make that happen.

But even that was months away. Fortunately, our line of gourmet mixes had already taken off, which counterbalanced the loss a bit. A few years earlier, Sam had helped found the Mississippi Specialty Foods Association. This proved to be a real asset in marketing. Our first product was our Rushing Wine Muffin Mix. These were served with every plate at the tea room, so I guess one could say our (good) reputation preceded it. It was an instant hit. Within a year, we had added our Oyster Mushroom Soup Mix, Southern Fried Chicken Mix, Gourmet Cheese Grits Mix, and Wassail Spice Blend. These were soon followed by a line of gourmet wild game mixes, including those for venison, fish, and dove and duck, all packaged in camouflage bags.

Unconstrained by the laws that severely limited our wine sales out of state, these products were soon available from coast to coast. We rented permanent space in the Dallas World Trade Mart and pitched our products every summer at the Fancy Foods and Gifts Market. Since my sister and her family lived in Dallas, we always took the kids with us. The Agnews entertained them in fine style while Sam and I were at the DTM, introducing them to such intoxicating venues as Six Flags, fancy malls, and water parks. Sam has never been amused by amusement parks, so this worked out especially well for him.

The exposure in Dallas proved to be most productive, as companies such as the Bass Pro Shop in Missouri and the Biltmore Estate in Asheville, North Carolina, picked up our products. Our gourmet mixes helped that summer, but they were not enough to carry us through the tremendous loss of wine we had suffered. We needed to make some money if we wanted to survive, and we needed to do it fast. I brainstormed other ideas, including catering, but with two small children at home and a business to run, that just didn't seem feasible. So, I set out to do something I had been contemplating for a while—writing a cookbook featuring all the recipes from Top of the Cellar Tea Room.

I had received a lot of help in collecting these recipes. From time to time, customers sat down, then handed me a favorite they thought might work well at the tea room. These "receipts," as they were often called in the South, were invariably handwritten on index cards. I was always grateful for their recommendations and used many of them at the tea room. Never did I receive a recipe that called for potatoes, however. And never was a potato in any form served at the tea room. The Mississippi Delta was big rice country and many of my patrons were beneficiaries of that fine crop. I was determined to respect their allegiance.

As word trickled out about my plans for the cookbook, some of my customers expressed concern, saying that my recipes should remain secret, that people may make them at home instead of coming to the tea room, and that my business may suffer as a result. While their hearts were certainly in the right place, I didn't think this was likely. I knew that the culinary skills most of these ladies possessed far surpassed my own. While my recipes were reliable and good, they were hardly indecipherable—a can of mushroom soup, half a cup of cheese, all the usual suspects one finds in a tasty Southern dish.

Still, I had learned by then that it was always a good idea to listen to my customers, so the next week I called one of them to get his thoughts on my writing a cookbook. His family had owned and operated a famous Italian restaurant in Memphis since the turn of the century. I was interested in what he had to say, as he had written a cookbook just two years earlier, *Wining & Dining with John Grisanti*, and I was curious to learn how it had affected his restaurant.

"Di, I had the same concerns when we first considered writing a cookbook, but the opposite has occurred," Mr. Grisanti said when I ran my idea past him. "Instead, my business has increased tremendously,"

"Interesting . . . ," I said. "Why do you think that happened?"

"Well, I believe releasing the cookbook provided the best advertising I've ever had, if you want to know the truth. Folks have told me when they try my recipes in their own kitchens, it just reminds them of Grisanti's—the ambience, the food, the service. And that makes them want to come back."

I considered what he was saying, and it certainly made sense. I was excited by Mr. Grisanti's insight, and not just because he owned one of the best restaurants in the mid-South; he was also an entrepreneur of the first rank. A decade or so before, he had broken the world record for purchasing the most expensive bottle of wine in history, a Chateau Lafite 1864, for $18,000. He broke it again in 2005 with his purchase of an 1822 Chateau Lafite Bordeaux; he paid $31,000 for that one. But Mr. Grisanti did not purchase these wines for personal consumption or even investment purposes. He immediately donated both to fundraisers for St. Jude's Children's Hospital in Memphis, raising over $100,000 at just one of the events. Big John Grisanti was as kind as he was astute, which is why I sought his opinion on the cookbook idea.

Mr. Grisanti confirmed my belief that the food was only one of the attractions to the tea room; the biggest was the atmosphere of cheerful rapport that existed within those walls. It was the people who made Top of the Cellar special, he said, and publishing my recipes would only enhance the business and broaden the base. I knew he was right. I loved it when my regular customers brought friends and family from far-off places in for lunch. Watching the look of pride on their faces as they showed them around the winery and tea room was a source of joy for me. One such customer especially comes to mind when I reflect on those moments.

Sis was a steady tea room patron from Drew, Mississippi, which was about nine miles further down the road. She and her lively group of friends were always a welcome sight as they came through the front door and headed straight for the private dining room and its table for eight. One day Sis brought two of her young grandsons in to tour the winery and have lunch. These lads were from New Orleans and, if memory serves, average in behavior—not too rowdy, courteous, certainly. They sat patiently, nibbling at their food and calculating, as all kids do, how much healthy stuff they were required to eat in order to qualify for dessert. I also recall that they had several large wine muffins each, along with a whole lot of butter.

The reason these little boys stand out in memory is because their father had been a famous quarterback at Ole Miss. I had watched him play at the Sugar Bowl in 1970, when Ole Miss went up against third-ranked Arkansas Razorbacks. It was an interesting New Year's Day in many respects. As I sat in Tulane Stadium in New Orleans with my mother, father, brother, and sister, I realized none of us knew which team to cheer for. While both of my siblings were recent graduates of Ole Miss, Mama had been a cheerleader at the University of Arkansas in 1936 and '37 and was a huge Razorback fan. To complicate things even further for her, she had gotten her master's degree from Ole Miss six years earlier. She presented quite the conundrum, turning heads as she wore her Razorback hog hat and yelled Hotty Toddy, Ole Miss's historic signature football cheer. The game ended in an upset, with Archie and his team winning, 27–22. He then went on to become the quarterback for the New Orleans Saints.

I remember thinking as I waited on Sis and her grandsons that it must be difficult to follow in the footsteps of someone as athletically gifted as their father. I always worried about things like that back then, and I felt kind of sorry for them. But those two little boys, Peyton and Eli Manning, did pretty well for themselves. Peyton won two Super Bowl championships, and so did Eli. Of course, of the two, former Broncos quarterback Peyton is my favorite, as our son Matt has always been a loyal Broncos fan. As a young boy, he parked himself in front of the TV every Sunday when the Denver team was playing, watching with the intensity reserved only for video games in today's world. Matt later ran the replay footage on the Jumbotron at Mile High Stadium for a couple of seasons when he was a journalism major at the University of Colorado. But as I said, Peyton and Eli turned out just fine, despite those big shoes to fill. I guess I needn't have worried about those sweet little boys after all.

Work on the cookbook began in earnest that summer, just one of many efforts we made to get back on our feet. During the day, we conducted business as usual. Liv walked in each morning to tend the children just as I walked out to tend the steady stream of customers who came through the winery and tea room. Business was brisker than ever, with the place booked to capacity every day. Our gourmet food line was also doing well, and it began to feel as though we may survive the duration until our new wines were ready for sale. Each day, after the last customer left, I sat at one of the tables with a glass of tea and typed out recipes for the cookbook, carefully adjusting the measurements to serve eight rather than thirty. Shirley often stayed as well, editing my work and finding mistakes here and there. I clearly recall those days, with the air conditioner humming as she and I worked in comfortable silence. It felt good to be doing something novel and productive, and I found my flow as the cookbook took shape.

With a little help from my friends, I located a publisher in Memphis who was ready to work with me, and her guidance led me to the finish line in early August. I asked my brother to shoot the cover photo of me on the front porch of the tea room and another of our young family for the back cover. I chose colors and artwork for the book. I wrote the dedication (to my parents) and the foreword and helped Sam with an amusing section on how he coordinated the winemaking process around his hunting schedules. With one last proofread by Shirley and me, I slipped the final draft into the mailbox at the Merigold Post Office and crossed my fingers.

Since there was no wine in the cellar that summer to work on, and nothing for us to bottle and ship, Sam also searched for new ways to fill his days. He got up early each morning and worked in the vineyard for a while. He continued his research on nouveau wines and began designing a new label featuring the blues singers of the Delta. But the activity he found most gratifying was his new love of glassblowing.

Sam had always wanted to be an artist, but family expectations had steered him into agriculture. He graduated with degrees in soil science and chemistry, but his heart was always, and still is, in art. He had been reading of late about an interesting new artist in Jackson, a glassblower named Susan Ford, and he became intrigued by her story. After multiple conversations on the phone and a few visits, she and he became fast friends. With her help, he began researching how to build a furnace and where to buy glass, color, and equipment for his new interest. He hand-built a primitive furnace and annealing oven in the warehouse and outfitted it with the bare necessities of glassblowing. A couple of months later, he blew his first piece of glass. He was smitten. Sam, too, had found his flow.

CHAPTER 17

Living by the Sword

November 4, 1990
Greenwood Commonwealth
Greenwood, Mississippi
The Good Life—Family Living Section

The Delta doesn't fade in the fall; it blossoms. Or, as Sam Rushing said, it "cools off and catches its breath."

The Delta days passed slowly for us that summer, as the humidity level and temperature locked arms and rose in tandem, both topping ninety on their respective gauges. Huge water moccasins slid from the cypress trees behind our house, slithering into our yard in their search for small prey. Lethargic red wasps constructed intricate nests under the eaves of our front porch, despite our painting the ceiling "haint blue" to keep them, and evil spirits, at bay. As Spring wrapped up her annual gig, the waters of the bayou surrendered their muddy brown hues and channeled cool green water instead, announcing, "Summer's here!" Beavers swam over from the vineyard side to the shore just below our house and built clever little dams that would likely be taken out by rotted tree stumps making their way to the Sunflower River.

Early that summer, I happened to be near the bayou's edge with the children, watching some industrious beavers as they constructed a small dam. They laughed as they watched the sleek little creatures grab the branches between their buck teeth and swim with them over to our side. I looked upstream and saw a clump of detritus headed straight for the little structure, and I picked up a stick to try to divert its path. Unsuccessful, I watched sadly as the new dam was washed away in the swift current. The next day, the beavers were back at work at the same spot again, seemingly undeterred by the previous day's setback. There was a lesson there somewhere, I felt certain.

This was the time of year when crickets sang all day long across the flat terrain of the Mississippi floodplain, and lightning bugs took over the landscape as darkness approached. Each night, mamas and grandmas across the Delta helped children poke holes in the shiny brass lids of old canning jars that would house these marvelous little neon-enhanced friends, caught gently in small palms. Cradling the empty jars in their laps, children patiently sat on their front porches, watching and waiting until the first twinkling lights appeared over the grass. As the night grew darker, so did the number of tiny sparks piercing the blackness of the gardenia-scented yards, hundreds of them blinking on and off to their own rhythm. Even the allure of television could not compete with the wonder of watching these bright little insects flitting about, twinkling in the twilight after a long day. And just before the lights went out for bed, the lightning bugs were set free once again, unharmed, to repeat the same age-old dance the very next evening.

Summers in Mississippi always made me feel as though I were a tiny creature living inside an enormous emerald terrarium, ripe with dense foliage, moist air, and strange critters. Everything in nature loomed larger during those hot months, and life beneath the Delta Dome became stifling, almost suffocating. People grew irritable as the heat and humidity escalated, and it seemed to me that the Delta itself transformed into a large, dysfunctional family whose members grudgingly loved each other, despite their individual proclivities.

At the winery that summer, Sam and I resolved to remain positive, hoping that Ray would soon be sleeping in prison instead of just
across the river. We were grateful that he had been indicted quickly
by the grand jury in May. The trial was scheduled for some time late
fall or early winter, and the consensus in the Delta was that with
all the evidence, and even a confession, he would be put away for a
while. The Mississippi State Penitentiary, in Parchman, Mississippi,
was located nearby, less than twenty miles from our home. This was
the same prison that later became famous in the Coen Brothers'
film, *O Brother, Where Art Thou?*, a sad depiction that was not far
from the truth. It would not be much of a journey for Ray, literally
or figuratively, were he to be found guilty and sent there, and our
friends and customers talked of little else.

One afternoon at the tea room, our insurance agent, the same
gentleman who had generously offered to testify that we had no
insurance to cover the losses we incurred, came to eat at the tea
room. I thought it was odd that he was alone, as he usually brought
his wife or clients with him. He sat down, took off his hat, and looked
me straight in the eye.

"Di, I am sorry to say that I paid for Ray's defense today," he
said. I looked at him, literally speechless. Surely, I thought, I had
misunderstood.

"Ray filed a claim on a tractor of his that caught on fire last
month," he continued. "While we are sure he set it, we couldn't prove
it. I wrote him a check for $35,000 this morning. Hardest thing I
ever had to do."

Water pitcher in hand, I slowly sat down at the table with him,
stunned, unable to fathom the enormity of this news. I tried to col-
lect myself as I realized my customers were watching with deep
concern, forks in midair, silent as sentinels. After a moment, I stood
up and went straight to the kitchen, where I remained until the last
customer was gone. Roberta, Flo, and Shirley were also appalled by
the news, but somehow, they summoned the gravitas it took to carry
on. I, on the other hand, was a hot mess. When I told Sam about

the conversation with the agent later that afternoon, I expressed my astonishment and rage at Ray's getting away with such blatant insurance fraud. I was spilling over with what my Baptist Sunday School teacher had always termed "righteous indignation." Sam, on the other hand, didn't seem a bit surprised.

"Ours is a legal system, Di, not a justice system," Sam responded. "We need to remember that."

Later that summer, our phone at the house rang one evening. These were the days before caller ID, so one can imagine Sam's surprise when the twangy voice on the other end was that of Ray's father, Emmitt.

"Sam, this here's Emmitt Russell." Sam waited silently for him to continue.

"I want you to drop the charges on my boy. He's sorry for what he done and he don't need to go to Parchman for it."

"That's not going to happen, Emmitt," Sam replied. Few people understood that we were not the parties who were formally pressing charges, although we certainly would have if given the opportunity. Bolivar County had this honor, and the State and Feds were considering it as well, as losses were incurred by both the State and the Bureau of Alcohol, Tobacco and Firearms. When our wine went down the drain, so did a lot of potential tax revenue. We were dissuaded by them from hiring an attorney to represent our interests; the District Attorney's office was assigned that task.

When it became clear to Emmitt that no charges would be dropped, his demeanor changed instantly. Supplication morphed into intimidation. He ranted for a full minute about how sorry we would be, ending the monologue with a bizarre threat. "You just remember this, Mr. Rushing," he said ominously. "It ain't over 'til the fat lady sings." We never really understood why he chose that particular aphorism to make his point; perhaps its crudeness appealed to him on some level.

Soon after that sinister phone call, fall arrived, and it was time for Lizzie and Matt to begin third and first grade, respectively. We were ready for the change in routine, as young families are everywhere that time of year. School supply lists were reviewed with anticipation and each item was chosen carefully. In the last week of August, school started, and the old carpool ritual began once again. Each morning, the kids hugged Sassy goodbye and Sam drove them about a mile to our neighbors' house. Mary Beth, who worked at a bank in Cleveland, then drove our two and her three children the remaining twelve miles to school. I picked all of them up at 3:30 and brought them home. On Friday afternoons, I treated everyone to snow cones at the local drive-in, a tradition that brought a great deal of pleasure. This was our third year carpooling and driving home together each day provided fun for the kids and convenience for the parents.

On the afternoon of the third day of school, I planned the menu for the next week at the tea room and got into my steamy car to go to pick up the five children. Fiddling with the air conditioner, I turned right onto the country road that led three miles west to Highway 61, the same country road that the Russell family lived on, just left of our turnoff. About a mile down the road, I noticed a car coming up behind me very quickly. I studied the rearview mirror as it hurtled towards me, going much faster than the speed limit allowed. As it came closer, I saw that the car was large. Old. Green. It was Ray.

Windows down, he pulled up to my left on the road, his car inches from mine, loud music blaring from his radio. Panicking, I glanced over at him. The menacing smile on his face as he looked at me sent a chill down my spine. In a desperate attempt to lose him, I accelerated quickly, then braked suddenly, but Ray maintained a steady pace with me. I slowed down, he slowed down. I sped up, he gunned his motor, laughing and staying right by my side. After a couple of minutes of this terrifying game, Ray suddenly whipped his car around mine and slowed to about ten miles per hour. I hit the brakes hard, my heart pounding and my hands tightly gripping the steering wheel. It was a lonely road, with only one house on the whole three-mile stretch. Should I stop? Should I try to turn around?

As these considerations bounced about my brain, I continued to drive slowly behind him, leaving plenty of space between us. I was close enough, however, that I could see his arm resting on his open window in the sun. I could see his greasy hair flying around his head. And I could see he was enjoying this dangerous romp, adjusting his rearview mirror for effect and taking frequent drags off whatever it was he was smoking. Finally, he reached the highway and took a right, flipping me off out the window as he drove towards Merigold.

I approached the intersection slowly, watching Ray's old green car continue north. I took a deep breath to calm myself, turned south, and pulled into the first place I thought was safe. I sat in the parking lot of a gas station, shaking so hard my teeth were rattling. I was furious. I pounded the steering wheel repeatedly, shouting "Son of a bitch!"

Sitting there, I made a decision. I started the car, put it in Drive and pulled back onto the highway. I collected the kids from school and sang and laughed with them all the way home. After I got Lizzie and Matt settled in front of the TV, I picked up the phone and told Sam to meet me in the back yard. I told him to bring his 44-caliber pistol. I told him he was going to give me a refresher course on how to shoot.

Still shaking, I fixed myself a glass of tea, went to Lizzie's room, and found some poster board under her bed. Sassy watched as I took a few magic markers from the desk drawer and sat cross-legged on the bed, energized by the powerful adrenaline still surging through me. I carefully outlined a target, four progressively larger black circles surrounding a big red one in the center. I resisted the strong temptation to personalize the bullseye. I went to my bedroom, quickly shed my tea room clothes and shoes, and put on shorts and a tank top. I looked in the mirror and saw a freaked out, thirty-something-year-old woman staring back at me. She looked high, and slightly insane. Sassy, tail between her legs, regarded me warily as I tied my tennis shoes. I looked into her brown eyes. She ducked her head, carefully studying this sea change in my demeanor. "It's okay, Sassy," I assured her. "It's still me."

Slinking behind me, she followed me back to the living room and took her place between the kids on the sofa. Taking a thumbtack from the bulletin board in the kitchen, I headed to the back yard, closing the door softly so as not to arouse their interest.

Easing down onto one of the dusty seats of the swing set, I contemplated where to place my homemade target in the dense woods behind our house. I heard a woodpecker hard at work in the bayou about a hundred feet below, quickly answered by a barn owl close by. I swatted at a huge mosquito on my calf and missed. The sweat on the outside of my ice-cold glass of tea mimicked that on my arms and legs as I surveyed the forest for the right tree for my target. There were dozens of old oaks and cypresses to choose from, each surrounded by a thick undergrowth of bamboo. High above, healthy kudzu vines wended a random path through the treetops, bridging the lush canopy. I was not moved by their exotic beauty, however; I knew them too well. Introduced in the Delta as a deterrent to erosion decades earlier, these hearty plants grew over a foot a day. Later described as "the vine that ate the South," they invaded the forests of Mississippi and beyond, slowly robbing them of sunlight and nutrients and leaving huge dead trees in their wake.

Sipping my tea, I looked up and pondered the delicate kudzu tendrils hanging from cypress branches, light green curls gently swaying in the breeze. They looked as though they were patiently awaiting the opportunity to seize, seduce, and strangle their unsuspecting hosts. The ancient trees seemed eager to embrace these vines in a naive attempt to connect, unaware that these beautiful creepers, while appearing friendly, were, in fact, lethal. Nature imitating man, I thought to myself. Studying the towering cypresses, hundreds of years old, I wondered how much longer they could survive in their beautiful home.

Soon, I heard Sam's truck on the gravel in front of the house. I ain't gonna lie—Sam wasn't too keen on my idea, even after I told him about Ray's stalking me that afternoon. He was furious, he was worried, and he was trying to determine the best way to handle the situation. This time we did report the incident to the sheriff. But Sam made it abundantly clear that he did not think that my becoming a pistol-carrying carpooler was the solution. He probably had good reason to doubt my plan; I didn't have a good record when it came to shooting a gun. But I had made up my mind.

I got off to a good start the first time I held a gun, not long after we graduated from Mississippi State. Some friends had brought their clay pigeon thrower to our house to shoot targets over the Sunflower River at sunset. It was a "Hold my beer and watch this" kind of evening and I hit the first two targets with my first two shots. Beginner's luck soon played out, however, and the allure quickly faded. The following year, I got fed up with a mouse that scurried across the kitchen floor a few nights in a row. I got Sam's pistol and shot up the baseboard beyond repair. A few years after that, I shot at Sam when he pulled into the driveway late one night. He was hunting at the club, and I wasn't expecting him until the next day. Thankfully, predictably, I missed.

Still, I didn't see how any of this had anything to do with what I was asking of him now. He had to admit that I needed some way to protect myself. I had responsibilities that required my driving to town alone every afternoon and until the trial, Ray was likely to be on that road. It was a scary situation, but I was damned if I was going to hide under the bed until December, when the trial was set to begin. I hit a few targets in the back yard, reloaded the gun, and stashed it under the driver's seat of my car. For the first time in my life, I religiously locked the car when I wasn't personally sitting in the driver's seat. I knew the dangers of carrying, but I also knew the dangers Ray posed those days. It was a precarious balance.

To make matters worse, it was just one week after this incident on the road that Big Tom, Sam's grandfather and the winery's ninety-two-year-old benefactor, passed away. He was sharp to the very end, but completely broken about the events of that year. I have no doubt they contributed to his rapid physical decline. As the old African proverb states, "When an old man dies, a library burns to the ground." With him went memories of growing up dirt poor in the Delta, learning to speak French during the Great War from his beautiful mademoiselle, cruising the turn rows in dusty cotton fields looking for bootleggers, and enjoying a beer with a blues player in some honky-tonk in the 1930s. He would have loved his funeral, though. It was rife with rich stories about his life, which had begun in obscurity in the nineteenth century and ended in modest fame near the end of the twentieth. He had often boasted of seeing Halley's comet twice in his lifetime, first at the age of twelve and again at the age of eighty-eight. His was a life to be proud of.

Shortly before he passed away, Big Tom told me that he would send an angel to watch over us after he was gone. It had been a tough year, after all, the year our wine flowed into the Sunflower River. Two days after the funeral, Sam's grandmother called and asked me to pick up a package at Sears that she had ordered a week or so before his death, a shoe organizer of some sort for her closet. I loaded the box into my car and took it to her. Still very sad and a bit distracted, we removed the staples and shook out the contents. Out of the box fell not a shoe rack, but a large, three-foot-tall plastic angel, the kind typically displayed in front yard nativity scenes at Christmas, kind of tacky, truth be told. Puzzled, we looked at the box, clearly marked "Shoe Organizer."

Frustrated, I went back to Sears to return the angel and reorder the rack. When I got there, the clerk told me that the paperwork reflected exactly what we had purchased, a shoe organizer, with the order number clearly stated. When I pulled the angel from the box, she was as confused as I was, apologizing and saying she would place the order again. Together we looked through her inventory catalog to see how much she should credit me.

"Well, I'll be," she muttered. "This just doesn't make any sense." She continued to flip through the pages, looking for the order number, but no item even came close to matching our surprise arrival that morning.

Suddenly, I remembered Big Tom's promise to send us an angel after he died. I knew right then that there was no way I was parting with this plastic harbinger of hope. I took a deep breath.

"Look, you're going to think I'm crazy, but I've decided I want to keep it," I said. "How much do I owe you?" The clerk looked up from the catalog, a puzzled expression on her face. A Christmas angel was hardly a rational substitute for a shoe rack.

"Well, sure, if you want it . . ." she replied. "I have no idea what to charge for it, though," she continued. "There's no listing for it here. So just take it, I guess." I picked up my huge plastic angel, sans box, carried her out to the car, and drove off, brainstorming logical explanations for this bizarre turn of events. Even now, I don't quite know what to make of this story.

Word soon got out about Big Tom's angel, and one November morning I opened the Memphis *Commercial Appeal* to find an article about it by renowned journalist Rheta Grimsley Johnson.

Titled "Maybe Big Tom came through on his angel promise," it read in part:

> . . . Sam's grandfather, Big Tom Rushing, always called Diane his little angel, don't you know. He promised he would send an angel down to protect Diane after he died.
>
> Big Tom did die in September, and yes, he sent an angel.
>
> I get a little carried away in the Delta. I admit it. Where others see a landscape flat as a Monopoly board, I anticipate the longer sunset. Where others complain of the monotony of the farmland, I see oceanic rhythms in the black and endless fields. There is simply a magic about the place that defies description.
>
> In the Delta I'm a sitting duck for stories about angels. . . . And if the angel came COD from Sears, well, that's just more meat to the mystery. (*Commercial Appeal*, November 23, 1990)

Big Tom, it seemed, was still making front page, above the fold, even after his death. The plastic angel later moved with us to Colorado, where I like to think she looks over us to this day.

It would be difficult to overstate the shadow that fell over us that summer and fall. On days when we least expected it, we would see Ray or his father on the road, or in the store, or at the gas station, and once again, we would be thrown into emotional turmoil. Merigold was a small town with about seven hundred people; it was not a place where one could easily avoid others when conducting daily business. Tension was a constant in our lives. Days were difficult and nights were nightmarish. Ray continued to taunt me at every opportunity he found me driving alone. Twice more that fall, I found him parked down the road, waiting for me to pull out to pick up the kids from school. Both times, he tailgated me for a minute, then whipped around in front and slowed to a creeping pace. The second time, I reached under the seat for my pistol just as he sped past me. He must have figured out what I was doing that time, as he never approached me on that road again.

A coward, Ray didn't stalk Sam as he did me, but Sam wasn't completely spared from the threats either. One day in October, he picked the kids up from school in Cleveland. As he pulled under the canopy, the teacher on duty greeted him cheerfully and herded Matt and Lizzie towards his truck. After loading them up, he began to pull away and saw Ray standing near the exit by his car, arms crossed, looking directly at him with the same creepy smile we had both come to loathe. He immediately got into his car and sped away, kicking up dust and alarming everyone within sight.

Of course, we reported it, and of course, nothing was done. No crime had been committed, after all. Like people everywhere who live daily alongside threatening players in their lives, nothing can really be done until it's, well, until it's too late. And as they know too well, restraining orders often do more harm than good. So, we did what others living under the shadow do: We exercised caution, and we waited for the trial.

The trial—in my mind, its possibilities grew into this miraculous panacea that would give us our old lives back, intact, unscathed. It loomed large behind every setback, waving its arms in the background and shouting, "I'm coming! Hang on! We got this!" I recognize now that this was a dangerous self-delusion. In mentally labeling the trial as "The Solution" and Ray as "The Monster," I was objectifying them, reducing the threat and giving myself permission to forget about the rest of the terror-filled fabric of our lives. I dismissed important epiphanies from earlier that year. I "forgot" that since March 28, the day we fired him, every negative thing that had happened to Ray was, in his mind, directly our fault. I failed to remember that his world had collapsed after losing his job and exacting revenge. I let slip from memory the knowledge that he had lost face, and that one's loss of dignity often provides a springboard for violence. I placed all my hopes on the trial, and the court date became my nexus to normality.

It was during this time that I began to notice a change in Sam. At night, as we watched TV after the kids went to bed, I often found him staring off in deep concentration, thinking thoughts he had no intention of sharing with me. I saw emotions of all brands play across his young face—anger, fear, sadness, questions. When I asked what he was thinking, he quickly reassured me that it was nothing, that he was just thinking about how good it would be when it was all over, and we could resume our lives with Ray tucked away in prison. But I worried about what he was thinking, what he was planning in the event that things went south. I knew he wasn't the type of man to allow his family to become a target.

And while we both hoped that justice would come that year, we also knew deep down that any sentence Ray received would some-day be completed, that even in the best-case scenario, we would be living out our later years with him and his father right across the river. We also realized that any little tricks he may learn from his stint in prison would likely further threaten our family. I understood these circumstances, internalized the darkness they represented, and dreaded the future. I just didn't know what to do about them. Except wait for the trial.

CHAPTER 18

House Specialties

October 21, 1990
Greenwood Commonwealth
Greenwood, Mississippi
1990 cooking school to be Nov. 8
By Susan Montgomery

The seventh annual Greenwood Commonwealth Cooking School will feature Merigold winery chef Diane Rushing at 7 p.m. Thursday, Nov. 8, at Greenwood High School auditorium. The public is invited at no charge.

Mrs. Rushing has operated the Top of the Cellar Tea Room at the Winery Rushing for seven years. She and her husband Sam have been in the winemaking business in Merigold for 13 years.

Mrs. Rushing is known across the Delta for the fine, fresh food and inventive menus that she serves at Top of the Cellar Tea Room. The restaurant was begun as an accommodation for visitors who regularly tour the winery and as a showcase for the Rushing wines, but it has also become a draw in itself, routinely luring return customers.

. . . Mrs. Rushing will discuss cooking with wine while she prepares some of the favorite dishes from the tea room. The recipes, which will be available to the cooking school audience, are also included in her soon-to-be published cookbook, "House Specialties of Top of the Cellar Tea Room."

I walked onto the stage of the brightly lit auditorium with its four hundred occupants and thanked the organizers of the 1990 Greenwood Commonwealth Cooking School for inviting me as their guest speaker. With Sam beside me, I was there to demonstrate a few recipes from my new cookbook, *House Specialties of Top of the Cellar Tea Room*, which had just been released earlier that morning. It had been an exhausting day already, and I was quite apprehensive about being touted as a "chef." Nothing was further from the truth, in my mind. I wasn't afraid of the public speaking piece; I had addressed larger groups throughout the years at Lions and Rotary Club Conventions and the like. But I had never done a cooking demo. Still, I had six thousand cookbooks to sell, so I summoned my courage and accepted the invitation. After a quick demonstration on wine glazed carrots, I began my instruction on how to create a truly magnificent chocolate cheesecake, one of my favorites at the tea room.

"The first step is to open a bag of Oreos, which will be crushed, mixed with melted butter, and used for the crust. It is very important, however," I added with gravity," that you set one cookie aside first."

I then went through the steps of the recipe, finally pouring the creamy chocolate batter into the cookie-lined springform pan. I showed them a finished version I had made the day before, beautifully garnished with whipped cream and fresh cherries. Smiling, I asked if there were any questions. One lady, a good customer from Greenwood, raised her hand.

"Di, why did you set aside that extra cookie?" she asked.

"Oh, that," I said. In answer, I took a bite of the cookie. "That's for you to eat when you're finished. This damn cheesecake has to sit overnight in the refrigerator. That's the only hard part about this recipe."

It's easy to write a cookbook when you already have the recipes. The hard part is the marketing. After the demonstration, Sam and I sat at a table as I signed the first cookbooks we had presented for sale. We sold over three hundred that night, which was encouraging, but I still envisioned the hundreds of boxes sitting in the back of the winery. We had taken out a loan to pay for them, which weighed heavily on our minds. Our grape harvest had been good in September, but the nouveau wasn't quite ready for bottling yet. It looked like sales for the new vintage were about two weeks out. Simply put, we were broke.

The cookbook was ninety pages long and featured every recipe we used at the tea room. It was bound by a plastic spiral comb with the tea room's name printed along the spine. I was very proud of it. The recipes were simple to follow, so simple in fact that it was a bit embarrassing to see them in print. The pages were sprinkled with silhouettes of my grandmother's lace that were framed and hanging in the tea room, as well as personal notes about some of the recipes and famous quotes about wine. My first order from the publisher had been for three thousand copies, but at the last minute, after quite a few advance orders from bookstores in the area, I bit the bullet and doubled the order. I was far from certain that this had been a good call. That was a lot of books to sell.

The next day at the tea room, we placed sample cookbooks on each table for my customers to look at and hopefully buy. The sales were good, and we were heartened by them. My friends at Cotton Row Bookstore in Cleveland were my best supporters, ordering twenty cases at a time. The timing didn't hurt either, as the Christmas season was quickly approaching.

November of 1990 gifted us with happy days at the Winery Rushing. Like most, we began to get caught up in the holiday spirit and some of our fears subsided a bit. The kids were happy at school and our Sassy had matured into the most beautiful black Labrador Retriever one could hope for. Gentle in spirit, she was an integral part of the family. She went everywhere with us—to work, to the hunting club, and of course, to bed with the kids each night.

Towards the end of the month, we began bottling the nouveaus, which immediately became popular with their light, crisp bouquet. Our Magnolia line, a fruity white, looked especially promising. We couldn't keep up as orders from liquor stores throughout the state and Memphis, often called "the capital of North Mississippi," began pouring in. The seven-month dry spell of wholesale sales had whetted a few thirsts, it appeared. Sam and I were ecstatic as cookbooks flew out the door and wine orders soared. Dinners at the house became cheerful again and the pall, it seemed, had finally lifted.

The continued support from the community and customers was also extremely gratifying; everyone, it seemed, was happy that the winery and tea room had survived the setback. Over the summer, we had often found anonymous contributions towards "the cause," such as a hundred-dollar bill hidden under a placemat, or $200 stuck in the tip jar. Once, there was a nice gift certificate for a local dress shop, and another for a children's store. We never knew for sure who the donors were; it could have been any of our customers.

These kind acts served to fortify us until the early days of December, when we would face Ray Russell in the Bolivar County Courtroom. We knew he had hired two Delta lawyers for his defense, both paid for through his insurance claim filed earlier that year. One of them had an excellent reputation for winning defense cases; $35,000 bought a lot of lawyer back then. We had no idea what his strategy was, but we knew the charge was simple burglary. As hard as the sheriff's office tried, there just wasn't a sufficient charge for letting someone's entire livelihood go down the drain. Towards the first of December, as the trial date neared, trepidation set in once again.

CHAPTER 19

Trial and Error

December 5, 1990
Bolivar Commercial
Cleveland, Mississippi
Trial for suspect in winery vandalism begins
By Robert H. Smith

. . . *Russell, 28, is charged with burglarizing the Winery Rushing near Merigold the night of May 3, releasing thousands of gallons of native Mississippi wine into the Sunflower River. Russell allegedly took $401 in cash as well. Rushing had fired Russell in March.*

Without conceding he took money, Russell's lawyers agreed Tuesday their client emptied six wine vats into the river. They also agreed he broke into and vandalized the Top of the Cellar Tea Room that Rushing and his wife, Diane, operate in connection with the winery.

And Russell did it all because Rushing had asked him to a few days earlier, said Defense Attorney Willard McIlwain Jr. of Greenville.

In making his opening argument Tuesday afternoon, McIlwain told the jury Rushing wanted his business ravaged for insurance and tax reasons. Rushing promised to make the vandalism worth Russell's while by rehiring him, said McIlwain.

On the stand, however, Rushing took issue with the lawyer.

"First of all, I have no insurance on the loss we incurred," he said. "And I don't know what the tax people are going to do, if anything."

"If you (McIlwain) know anything about how I can get a tax write-off, please let me know."

The trial began on Tuesday, December 4. Immediately we began to see where the defense was going. According to Ray's attorneys, he did indeed destroy our businesses on that night in May, but he did so at our request, they said, for insurance money and tax write-offs. The fact that we had no insurance seemed to be irrelevant. Sam and I were sequestered during the trial, so all we heard about the proceedings that didn't involve our direct testimony was second-hand, but that was enough. We learned that Ray admitted to everything he did, except the actual crime he was being charged with, the theft of $401. But his lawyers set out to make the case that he did it as a favor to us.

It doesn't take much intelligence to recognize the convoluted logic inherent in Ray's defense, as outlined in their "sequence of events." First, they maintained, Sam and I spent fourteen years building two incredible businesses, with many plans for future expansion. Then we decided to destroy it all by asking Ray to let the wine go and vandalize the tea room for the insurance money. (Oops. . . . Forgot to take out that policy first.) But to make it plausible, we also asked him to kill our children's dog and shoot up our house. Then we fired him. Next, he was to come back about six weeks later to fulfill the rest of the agreement by letting the wine drain from the tanks and destroying the tea room.

"What was in it for Ray?" they posited. "He got to work at the winery again," they responded. According to the *Bolivar Commercial* (Smith, December 6, 1990), "Russell said from the stand Wednesday that Rushing promised to give him a job in return."

Before the trial started, we had begun to hear about prospective jurors who were being dismissed because they knew us personally or had visited the winery. Of course, we understood the concept of "jury of one's peers" and all, but finding twelve registered voters in Bolivar County who had never been to the winery had proved a bit difficult. After interviewing and dismissing well over a hundred individuals, twelve were chosen, eight women and four men. My friends in the courtroom that day told us that as the trial progressed, the circus quickly became less about the events at the winery and more of a discussion about the haves and the have-nots. It soon became apparent that the injustice of economic disparity was going to be the underlying premise of Ray's defense.

My time on the stand didn't help our case much. By then I was oh-so-tired of victimhood, and my testimony came across as defensive and angry. I was both, of course. I had worn my "Sunday Best" for the day, unaware of the financial angle that Ray's lawyers were planning to lay out. To hear them tell of it, Sam and I were shamefully wealthy and Ray, just a poor boy trying to make his way through this tough old world.

Jack, our long-time vineyard manager, was also called to testify. According to Smith's article on December 6, he

> told the jury Wednesday morning that Russell confessed he broke into the winery because he was mad at Sam Rushing.
>
> He said, "the boss called me a son-of-a-bitch and that was it," [Thomas] recalled Russell saying when asked why he was mad.

Smith continued, describing the closing arguments of Ray's defense:

> Additionally, (Defense Attorney) McDowell made his customary appeal to patriotism. McDowell told jurors he was proud to be an American. He reminded them that U.S. troops are in the Middle East now to protect the American way of life.
>
> Ranging back nearly 400 years, McDowell compared the Russells to the Pilgrim fathers, looking for relief from persecution by the rich and privileged. He told the jurors . . . to remember

the struggles of leaders like Fannie Lou Hamer and Medgar Evers when considering whether to convict Russell. (*Bolivar Commercial*, December 6, 1990)

Immediately following this charade, the jury was sent out of the courtroom to debate the case. During this time, Sam and I remained sequestered in the small, warm room just off the courtroom. We were shaken by the line of questioning about our asking Ray to destroy our own property, our (nonexistent) insurance policy, and baseless innuendo regarding our personal lives. We had been totally unprepared for any of that. And we didn't comprehend the legal tactics so powerfully employed that day: That by clouding the issues, creating chaos from a simple narrative, reasonable doubt could be cast. Ray's defense threw a lot at the wall that day. We would soon learn if any of it stuck.

But according to the *Bolivar Commercial*, the conversation in the courtroom between Ray's lawyer and the deputy sheriff was even more bizarre than the one Sam and I were having in the next room.

. . . While the jury deliberated, (Defense Attorney) McIlwain asked idly of a sheriff's deputy if the judge would sentence his client that afternoon. The deputy pointed out there was no guilty verdict yet. (Smith, December 6, 1990)

When the verdict came in about an hour later, we were back in the courtroom. The judge asked if the jury had reached a verdict and they said they had. He took the piece of paper, looked at it, shook his head slowly, and handed it back down. The verdict: Not Guilty.

I could not speak for anyone else in the courtroom in that moment, but the sense of betrayal and injustice rocked me to the very core of my soul. I doubled over from the immediate physical pain I felt in my stomach, the proverbial gut punch. Then I sat upright on the hard courtroom bench in my blue silk dress and my grandma's pearls and my new high heels, staring straight ahead in absolute disbelief, seeing nothing. I heard a cacophony of sounds around me as I and others tried to process what had just occurred. Our supporters sat stunned as Ray's small cadre rejoiced. His lawyers, somewhat reluctant recipients of Ray's and Emmitt's hugs and slaps on the back, slinked away from the angry stares of Bolivar County's best. Gradually, people approached us with words of sympathy compounded by disbelief. I sat perfectly still, looking straight ahead and saying nothing for a full ten minutes. If Ray was not guilty, I wondered, did that mean we were? And if so, guilty of what? And the most painful of all: Why had that jury believed him and not us?

As I sat there, I heard a voice behind me, breaking through the white noise in my head. "You told me to handle it," it said. "I'm handling it."

Stunned, I turned around to see who had spoken, but no one was there. To this day I am not sure what transpired in that moment, but whatever it was, it served to bring me back to the reality of the pandemonium in the courtroom. My good breeding surfaced again, and I made all the proper noises in response to the deluge of sympathy we received. According to the *Bolivar Commercial*, just before leaving,

> Sam and Diane Rushing, owners of the winery, thanked the District Attorney Laurence Mellon for his efforts in prosecuting the case, and asked for his prayers.
>
> "We lost seven months ago," Diane Rushing said moments later. "We lost when our wine went out into the river." (Smith, *Bolivar Commercial*, December 6, 1990)

And that was a fact.

For a long time, I beat myself up about the trial, holding myself partially responsible for its outcome. Like most people, I often have these insidious little mutterings in my head, keeping me humble, eagerly pointing out everything I have done wrong. Proponents of

Eastern philosophy call this cerebral noise the Human Ego. I call it "the Asshole in my Head," and it was hard at work as I second-guessed everything after the verdict, from trusting the justice system to wearing my hair up that day. But in retrospect, I believe some of the fault was in the egregious inadequacy of the charge itself: Burglary. Four hundred and one dollars—such a paltry sum for such a huge loss.

I suspect that the bulk of the blame, however, lay in the flagrant combination of naïveté and overconfidence on the parts of all the main players sitting on our side of the courtroom that day, me included, of course. There's no doubt that important balls were fumbled, and effective strategies were unexplored. Having been sequestered, Sam and I were largely unaware of the proceedings, and I remain puzzled today about how Ray and his lawyers pulled it off. What I do know is that we were in survival mode by the time we heard the words, "Not Guilty." Immediate suggestions of pursuing a civil trial or any other avenue of justice was just too big an ask. Maybe later, we thought, but not that day. That day we just wanted to go home.

CHAPTER 20

When Memory Refuses to Serve

The next four days were a blur. I got a script for antidepressants and refilled my sleeping pills for the fourth time. I relied on Sam and my tea room support group to shoulder all my responsibilities. I think I spent most of the time in bed. It would be disingenuous on my part to try to describe the events from December 6 to December 10. I don't remember a thing.

CHAPTER 21

Time to Go

December 13, 1990
Delta Democrat Times
Greenville, Mississippi
Shot puppy was final blow for Mississippi's 1st winery
By Sonya Kimbrell

The December day was bright and sunny, and the air was unseason-ably warm outside the Winery Rushing and Top of the Cellar Tea Room Wednesday.

Diane Rushing sat near the winery entrance, greeting customers with smiles and small talk as usual, going back and forth between the winery and the tea room.

Lizzie Rushing, 8, sat on top of the counter helping ring up pur-chases while winery employee James Harris offered samples of the various wines produced from the Rushings' 28-acre muscadine vine-yard near Merigold.

But if you leaned in a little closer, you'd hear Mrs. Rushing accepting condolences from friends and longtime customers; you'd see Harris have to tell a customer there were no more bottles of Magnolia to sell.

. . . Russell was acquitted last week by a Bolivar County Circuit Court Jury. . . . The experience of the trial left the Rushings dazed.

"We were the ones trying to prove our innocence, it seemed," said Mrs. Rushing.

But even that didn't make them want to leave. The decision to leave was made when the Rushings . . . found their black Labrador puppy, Sassy, shot through the heart and thrown into the trash. With two small children, Lizzie and 6-year-old Matt, to think about, the Rushings have decided to . . . start over in Colorado.

When I woke up on the morning of December 10, I knew I had to function again. I had an appointment in Memphis that afternoon with a specialist who had placed me on a clinical study several years earlier, and I could not miss it. I got up, dressed and fed the kids, and got them off to school. Sam's cousin Sara was covering for me in the tea room, as she often did, and Sam was driving us to Memphis.

As I picked up around the house and readied for the two-hour trip north, I heard Sam coming in the front door. I recall that things seemed to feel a bit brighter that morning, although we were still far from recovered from the shock of the verdict. After many tears and much discussion just after the trial, we predicted that Ray was going to react one of two ways: Either he would realize how lucky he was to be walking free, or he would interpret the "Not Guilty" verdict as a green light to do whatever else he wanted to us. Time would tell, I guess.

When I saw Sam's face, I knew he had chosen the latter.

"Jack just found Sassy, Di," he said. "She's been shot. . . . She's dead."

I had let Sassy out early that morning as was custom. Rarely did she go beyond the yard before whining to get back in. In my current state of mind, I had not realized she had been gone for a couple of hours. Stunned, I waited for the rest.

"He stuffed her in the garbage by the winery," Sam said. I knew who "he" was; everyone in the Delta would know who "he" was. Ray was back.

And just like that, so was the impenetrable darkness.

Neither of us said a word as we drove the first fifty miles or so to Memphis. There was nothing left to say. Sam was back in his "deep thoughts" mode, and I could tell by the determined look on his face that the wheels in his head were steadily spinning. I sensed that his was dangerous thinking this time around, one possibly involving violence of some nature, and that it would not end well for anyone. The justice system had failed us miserably, and even the loving support of those surrounding us would not protect us from the frightening specter of Ray at this point. Most disturbing perhaps, I felt that nothing I could say would change whatever decision Sam was contemplating.

Silently, Sam and I sped past cotton fields that had been picked clean and run-down sharecropper houses, smoke curling from their chimneys. Billboards advertising Camel cigarettes and car dealerships whizzed by as I pondered the Delta landscape out the window and wondered what to do next. Rusted cars littered small plots of land, and indifferent junkyard dogs watched us pass by. I felt as hopeless as they looked, wondering how we were going to move forward from this latest tragedy. It was depressing as hell.

Lizzie and Matt had already left for school by the time Jack had found our precious Sassy that morning. I searched my brain for the best words to break the devastating news when they got home that afternoon. Silently, I practiced different monologues to find the kindest, gentlest way to tell them, but none seemed even remotely adequate. The looks on their faces upon finding Socks earlier that year played a toxic loop in my head. I envisioned them standing by their swing set, watching as Sam dug yet another hole next to the graves of Oreo and Socks. I watched the makeshift memorial service unfold in my mind, four heads lowered as we ended yet another sad ceremony in our back yard.

Riding along, I asked myself how anyone could expect our children to bounce back from this, just one more terrifying event in the course of many during the past nine months. Could we really ask them to spend their childhood days in constant fear of the dangerous rednecks living just across the river? I wondered how we could convey to them the moral obligation of not striking back with violence, the only language Ray apparently spoke. And I wondered if passive resistance was, in fact, how I even wanted it to play out. I had no answers as the angels on my shoulders exchanged philosophical blows.

After half an hour or so, I suddenly looked across the front seat at Sam and blurted out something I didn't even know I had been thinking.

"Sam . . . we're moving," I said.

"What did you say?" he said with a jolt. I had startled him out of his dark reverie. He continued to gaze steadily down the straight black line called Highway 61. We had just passed the plaque commemorating the spot where a famous blues player, Robert Johnson, sold his soul to the devil. The legend goes that in exchange, the devil gave him the ability to play a mean guitar, right there at the crossroads of Highways 61 and 49. The improbable convergence of my bleak thoughts and this infamous intersection seemed significant somehow.

"We're moving," I repeated. "And I don't mean just down the road where he can find us again. We're moving to Colorado."

I don't know which of us was more shocked by the words spilling out of my mouth. I hadn't even considered the prospect of leaving before that moment. Since the trial, we had discussed how we were going to live with Ray back across the river; we had yet to figure that out. Security gates, metal fences, and burglar alarms were likely in our future. But we had never talked about just picking up and leaving. And why Colorado? I guess because that was where happy vacation memories were created. That, and it seemed so far, far away.

"What do you mean, we're moving?" Sam looked over at me, realizing that I was quite serious. His green eyes squinted as he studied my face carefully.

"I mean we're leaving. I don't intend to stay here and swap licks with Ray and his father for the rest of our lives," I said. We knew that the two of them had been celebrating day and night since his victory in court. We could hear the boozed-up festivities from our front porch. It was bizarre.

Immediately, I realized that the idea appealed to him. It was an electric moment. He had to be on board as much as I was, of course. Sam was third generation on the farm, and seventh generation Mississippian. This was no small thing. I wasn't even sure how I felt about the idea yet, but it quickly gathered legs in my mind as we drove north. I intuited that he was seriously considering the prospect. We rode in silence for a bit.

"Okay," he finally said, exhaling a long, pent-up breath.

"When?" I asked.

"Soon."

"How soon?"

"By the end of this year."

"As in three weeks?"

"Three weeks," he said.

As we explored the idea, we became more hopeful, more animated. Not happy, mind you, —far from that—but guardedly hopeful. For the first time in a long time, we felt that maybe, just maybe, we could live somewhere other than that place called Fear, that maybe we could find a spot on the planet where our babies could feel safe again. It didn't seem too much to ask.

By the time we got to Memphis, we had pretty much decided to stay open until Christmas Eve or so, then pack up and leave as quickly as possible. Much like our first year of marriage in Germany, we didn't know what we were going to use for money, but we did have faith in our ability to land on our feet again. We had "debts no honest man can pay" as Bruce Springsteen once described it, but Sam was already thinking of ways to address those as well. The previous year, the Mississippi Wildlife Federation had offered stellar prices to put some of the upper acreage aside for wetlands, so that was a good option, as it would cover the loan payments. As for what we would live on once we left, we had to give that a lot more thought.

Sitting on the white papered table at the hospital an hour later, my voice trembled as I told my doctor about our finding Sassy in our garbage that morning. He and I had established a comfortable rapport in the couple of years I had been seeing him, and we enjoyed catching up every six months when I came in for appointments.

A renowned specialist, he had seen a thing or two during his thirty years of practicing and teaching medicine, so I was a bit surprised when the color instantly drained from his face, and he slowly sat down on his black rolling stool. I then told him about our decision to leave. He was already familiar with our story, as were most in the area, but this genuinely rattled him.

"Jesus," he said, when I was finished.

"I know," I said. "I have no idea if this is the right thing or not, but I know we can't just be sitting ducks in our own home anymore. Somebody is going to get killed if we stay here. I don't know if it will be Ray or one of us, but someone will." I knew as I spoke these words that they were absolutely true. But God, I hated how melodramatic I sounded. Sam and I had become so weary of drama over the past nine months. We sat in silence for a few minutes.

"Well, Di, for what it's worth, I think you and Sam are doing the right thing," he finally said. "And while you don't realize it now, and I feel bad for saying it, this may have been the best thing that could have happened under the circumstances."

I knew he was right.

"He wouldn't have served more than a few years, even if he had been convicted," he continued. "And now . . . well, now you really don't have much choice, do you?"

With few exceptions, that seemed to be the consensus in the coming weeks, as word got out that we were closing the winery and tea room for good. Once again, customers were bringing us food and offering assistance. And once again, the media was at our front door. This time I was more prepared for the onslaught. I felt in control as I told reporters that we were closing up shop, moving to Colorado.

I was a bit afraid to give them the specifics, knowing Ray would be listening. Ostensibly, I was resolved. Internally, I was terrified.

Lizzie was excited about the prospect of moving to Colorado. She had always loved going there on vacation, either to Telluride or Durango. She looked at the bold move as an adventure. Matt was much more hesitant, however. All he thought about was leaving his friends and home for the Great Unknown. I remember Lizzie coaxing him to get on board with sweeping depictions of dude ranches and horses. But Matt was sad and didn't want to go. At times I felt just as he did; at others, I couldn't leave fast enough. But as the good Doc said, we didn't have much choice in the matter, and that was somewhat vindicating. Sam and I both knew that if we stayed, someone would likely pay the price with a lifetime sentence—or worse. There was no good choice, just varying degrees of bad ones. And so it goes.

CHAPTER 22

Standing on the Corner of Right and Wrong

December 1990
Commercial Appeal
Memphis, Tennessee
Winemaker's dreams end in sour grapes
By William Thomas

The days of wine and roses are over in Merigold, Miss., for Sam Rushing and his family.

On Thursday, he and his wife and two children plan to leave for a small town in Colorado where the 38-year-old pioneer winemaker will try to put behind him a dream that has become a spooky chiller. Rushing, the founder of Mississippi's first legal winery since prohibition, closed down operations on Friday after a long run of bizarre incidents that have included a burglary, the dumping of 8,000 gallons of wine into the Sunflower River, the killing of two dogs, the firing of a bullet through his roof and the creeping conviction that someone was going to get hurt if he stayed in Merigold.

"I feel like I'm in a no-win situation," said Rushing, who hung a "For Sale" sign on his vineyard, his winery and his gourmet restaurant . . .

(Sam said) he would throw in his dream for free.

Soon after we had made the decision to leave, told our families, and notified our friends, I began to doubt the whole idea. *What the hell are we doing?* I asked myself. *To our children, our families, our neighbors, and friends?* I felt as though I were skiing down a steep mountain, poles askew, totally out of control. I began to question who I was, what kind of a person I was. I decided I needed to think, or maybe rethink.

As a freshman at Millsaps College in Jackson, I had been a psychology major. I loved the field of study, but abandoned it early on for various reasons, not the least of which was that I thought I recognized myself in some of the case studies. Despite the shift to English major, however, I remained interested in psychology, studying what makes people tick. For entertainment, I often found myself reading old textbooks, perusing the latest Diagnostic Manuals, and poring over nerdy publications.

A few nights after Sassy was killed, as I lay in bed agonizing over the decision we had made and pondering its ramifications, I recalled reading about a phenomenon called "status quo bias." This term describes the strong desire of people to avoid change, even in untenable situations. There are a lot of logical explanations for this, including the facts that we usually find it easier to do nothing, that we tend to overvalue what has worked in the past, and that we feel more in control by sticking with the known, avoiding risk in the process. In other words, maintaining the status quo tends to be our default mode. And, it seems, the more options we have, the greater the tendency to leave things just as they are.

By this point, I was really second-guessing myself, an annoying habit that persists with me today. Keeping the status quo, I concluded, staying put and hoping for the best, might be the best course after all. What if we move to Colorado and fail miserably? What if we can't find a job? What if the children don't make new friends and cry themselves to sleep each night? Maybe the best decision was no decision. Except, I realized: Doing nothing is also a decision, even though it may not feel like one. And in our case, likely an unwise one.

Later that week, when everyone was asleep, I began making lists of all the pros and cons of leaving, even assigning numerical ratings of importance to each factor in two columns. I knew this was one of the most consequential decisions of our lives, and I wanted to get it right. But the numbers were not doing it for me. Around midnight on the second night of struggling with these hopelessly subjective "calculations," I considered how our decision to leave was affecting so many different people in so many different ways.

I thought first about Sam's grandmother who had just been widowed and depended on us for many of her day-to-day needs. I worried about Liv and Roberta and Jack, who had worked for us for so long. What would they do? Where would they find good employment with someone who loved and appreciated them as much as we did? I thought of my brother Nelson, who worked in nearby Leland as an electron microscopist for the USDA; his loving presence was such an integral part of our daily lives. And while my parents had retired and lived six hours away, I feared that I wouldn't be there when they needed me in the coming years as they grew older. We had always been close, and I felt that I owed them more than moving so far away. Most of all, I was tormented by the idea of ripping Lizzie and Matt from the only home they had ever known.

Frustrated, I threw the "pros and cons" charts into the trash. Chewing the end of my pencil, I pondered how I could better decide which course we should take. There had to be a way to quantify these factors, I reflected, some way to make sense of the endless stream of thoughts that had been skating through my conscience since we had decided to move.

Drawing on my English background, I began looking at the problem through the lens of a grammar conjugation chart, with first, second, and third person, singular and plural. Curiously, I chose the infinitive "to run" as I contemplated how this might work: I run, You run, He/she/it runs, We run, You run, They run.

On a new sheet of paper, I created the point-of-view chart, leaving large spaces under each of the six categories. As I worked on it, fascinating dynamics emerged. First person singular reflected me, of course, and how this decision would alter my life personally; similarly, first person plural represented my immediate family. Second person, singular and plural, was filled with the ramifications our decision would have on our friends, customers, employees, and community. Third person singular represented Ray; plural included his father.

It soon became apparent that Ray and his father stood to gain the most from a decision to cut our losses and move to Colorado. Not only would the notion of "winning" feed their obdurate egos, they could now remain comfortably in their rundown compound without the nuisance of having to plot further ways to terrorize us. (They transferred this hatred to their neighbors on the other side of them just a few years later. According to a friend, Ray "emptied his shotgun" into the cab of their truck one night, narrowly missing the driver. That family, too, decided to move away.) The irony wasn't lost on me that the morally right decision, to walk away, most benefited the one person who had forced that decision in the first place. And that the losers, on so many levels, were the members of my family.

As for the effect it would have on the community—second person plural—tangible evidence of this was pouring in every day from people all over the mid-South through correspondence and phone calls. Over a hundred cards and letters arrived within a few days of the news, most of which were sad but supportive. While I did not recognize many of the names, it was interesting to read the reactions of those whom I had known for many years. More than a few little old ladies expressed anger and outrage, some using surprisingly violent rhetoric. Sentiments such as, "The shocking outcome of your day in court has disturbed me greatly," to simply, "Please don't go," landed in our mailbox every day. Someone whom we had never heard of, a professor of Psychology from the University of Southern Mississippi, wrote:

> Mississippi will suffer from the loss of such fine people like you. It may be too late to dissuade you from leaving, but I would like to know if

you have any ideas as to how this gross miscarriage of justice could be addressed. I am willing to devote time and energy to this cause.

One of the most disheartening, however, was from an elderly customer from Marks, Mississippi, who wrote in her loving longhand:

> How I've agonized about choosing words to write to you two energetic, creative, hardworking, beautiful young people who have over the years filled a very special place in our hearts! To say that we, too, are heartbroken about the recent turn of events is a gross understatement. There is no way to tell you how much it has affected our spirit to realize that justice can so far miss its target and that innocent people like you can be victimized to the extent to which you have been. There aren't enough words of compassion to express our sorrow and concern and grief about the destruction of your beautiful dream. I'm sure it must be like the death of a loved one, for so much of your life went into the dream.

She went on to wish us the best, as did countless others. These letters went a long way towards healing our wounds, but they also made me question our decision to move even more. It seemed unlikely we would land in a place that surrounded us with such love.

A couple of the messages were somewhat less sensitive to our loss, such as this one from a bank president who lived on the other side of the county:

> . . . I realize that you have suffered a severe loss on account of the burglary and its after effects [sic]. Nevertheless you can overcome this calamity if you will just rearrange your affairs and stick to the matter. Count it as a Bad Crop and look forward to 1991.
>
> The farmers in this area had the same bad season but they are not "throwing in the towel."
>
> . . . Take out some burglary insurance or stock inventory insurance. I am sure it can be obtained.

Upon reading this letter, Sam and I were livid. Rearrange our affairs? A bad crop? Take out insurance? Jesus. Perhaps the banker's heart was in the right place, but his letter firmly reinforced our decision to leave as it spelled out so clearly how limited our options were. It bothered us no small bit that a few people may have looked at our leaving the Delta as "throwing in the towel." Running from one's problems is not acceptable—that is one of the cardinal rules of life. But knowing the rules is the easy part; it's knowing when the rare exceptions apply that it becomes a bit tricky. To my mind, prevention was not quite the same thing as running. Sam and I were being forced to determine on an elemental, primordial level which path was moral and which was not. I had navigated difficulty many times before, as has everyone, and as a rule I had chosen well. But this was different. This was a cognitive decision between doing the right thing or not doing it. This was saying it out loud. This was metadeciding.

I would be dishonest if I said the choice was easy, that nobility easily won the day. We loved our home and would have fought for it bravely had it not been for the very real threat to our family, and Ray had made it clear that his game was back on, full-court press. The only way to remove that threat was to "remove" the person who represented it. And no matter how we looked at it, that was, well, wrong.

Fortunately, I had developed some valuable strategies by then. I had learned to listen to my feminine instinct. I had learned to be still. During the previous months, this instinct had spoken up when I most needed an honest friend. While it was a bit short on specifics, it had always been spot-on. Sometimes it convinced me to act; other times, to watch and wait. In the rare instance that I denied its lead, when I refused to be still and know, the end game suffered. And now, it told me, it was time to go.

Sam and I knew that although we had never been ones to avoid confrontation when necessary, there was just too much to lose this time around. And sure enough, we were told a few days after we found

Sassy that an emboldened, drunken Ray Russell had been overheard at the liquor store muttering, "Them Rushing kids are next."

Remembering this, my heart pounded as I looked at the point-of-view chart one more time. I run, You run, He/she/it runs. There was only one fallacy in this conjugation: Everyone knew Ray wasn't running anywhere. Doing the right thing had never been quite so hard.

CHAPTER 23

Long List of Last Times

December 19, 1990
Bolivar Commercial
Cleveland, Mississippi

To the Bolivar Commercial:

Will you please accept this letter as a public farewell to Sam and Diane Rushing?

The Odoms are the Rushings' nearest neighbors to the south. We have watched in amazement and admiration as they clawed their way into making their dream for their farm come true. They are two of the hardest-working young people we have ever known. I remember the time of their first crushing of grapes. Sam made the comment that he wished he did not have to give up time from work to sleep. Few of us have ever worked so hard or with such vision.

The Rushings are producers; they are builders; they are contributors. They have brought positive attention, not only to Merigold and Cleveland but also to Bolivar County and the State of Mississippi. In an area that is generally looked down on for its poverty and crime, this success story is greatly needed.

Now, after fourteen years of back-breaking labor, they have become victims, not once but twice. Somehow, I feel that we should stand up in their defense, but my pen is the only weapon I have.

Sam and Diane, I want to say publicly that I and my family thank you for showing farmers that alternate ways of using the precious soil of this Delta land can be found. Thank you for proving that success is possible if one is willing to work hard. Thank you for the contributions you have made to your church and our community.

We cannot afford to lose bright, industrious, God-fearing young people like Sam and Diane Rushing. How sad the day when we can't protect them and help them to stay. How tragic that we who wish to speak out for them feel we do so at personal risk. God help us all.

Sincerely,
Mary Ann Odom (Mrs. Lee Odom)

The last week of operation at the winery was akin to the game of Whack-a-Mole. Just as I solved one problem, another one popped up. When that one was resolved, up popped one more right beside it. But it was a week of pleasant surprises as well. Lizzie's class had held their Christmas party earlier in the week and all the Secret Santa gifts had been addressed to her, per a successfully covert arrangement by the third grade earlier that week. Matt's first grade class and their teacher were in tears as they sang a song written just for him. Then they presented personal letters, written on their Red Chief writing tablets, straight from their six-year-old hearts. On December 23, the First Methodist Church in Cleveland held a huge reception in our honor to say goodbye. Letters and phone calls continued to pour in, first imploring us to stay, then concluding that perhaps it was, indeed, best to go. It was a mad, quicksilver junket, and it was exhausting.

By that time, over the phone, we had found a place to live in Norwood, about thirty miles from Telluride in southwest Colorado. The agent told us that the house was old and dark, but at $500 per month, it was all we could afford. We had friends who had moved from Mississippi to Telluride many years earlier. We had met them while at Mississippi State and visited them several times, on ski trips in the winter, and later when camping with the kids. She was a realtor and he was an ER physician; between them, they had found us a place to land and lick our wounds.

The plan was to pack and close up the winery and tea room by Christmas Day, then work on the house until we left on December 27. My parents had come down from Mountain Home to help out, as had other family members and friends. The last day at the tea room, December 21, fell on Roberta's birthday, which made the day even more poignant. The mood in the kitchen was a curious blend of fond reminiscence and debilitating defeat. As we worked, we knew we were doing everything for the last time. It was the last time Shirley whipped up fresh wine muffins, the last time Flo took the McCarty plates down and lined them up to serve, and the last time Roberta slid a chocolate pie into the oven.

In the dining room, where customers were packed in, it was more an air of anger tempered by loss. During the first seating at 11:30, the place was filled with teachers from the area celebrating the beginning of the holiday season, as had become the custom. Usually a rowdy bunch, they were quite subdued that day, lowering their voices when I approached and treating me as though I were a Faberge egg.

"Di, please be sure to send us your new address," they said.

"This is so wrong. We're gonna miss y'all so much," they said.

"We are so mad we could just spit!" they said. I floated through the first shift laughing at some of the exchanges and tearing up at others. While I understood their anger, I didn't really share it anymore. By then, I was in my reliable Di Rushing "Movin' On" mode. This propensity to put the worst behind me posthaste is neither admirable nor practical-it is just Denial dressed up fancy to look like Determination. Sometimes I do that instead of "deal." Sometimes I pay a high price for it. Nevertheless, a survival strategy it is, and one that I needed desperately that day.

The second seating at 1:00, however, was going to be the litmus test of my ability to don my big girl britches. I had saved this last dance for my favorite clientele when booking the reservations during the previous two weeks. As the teachers filtered out, a gradual stream of elderly, well-coiffed ladies and coat-and-tied gentlemen steadily made their way through the front door for their last lunch at Top of the Cellar. This tea room demographic was composed of retired Delta folk from all walks of life. Many had frequented our place nearly every week for over seven years, steadfast supporters patiently guiding me as I had grown as a young mother, a restauranteur, and a human being.

Over the years these fine people had given me treasured recipes to try, carefully written on index cards with precise measurements such as "butter the size of a small walnut." They had quietly informed me when a recipe didn't work and had loudly praised me when it did. They had brought tomatoes from their gardens, and they had complained when the air conditioner was set too cold. They had gifted me with books they thought I might enjoy and had scolded me when I wouldn't let them smoke at the table. They had erupted in utter delight when one day, six years earlier, one of them had discovered a clean baby sock lost in the folds of her linen napkin. (I always laundered them at home.) I was absolutely horrified when I saw the tiny blue sock, but they laughed and quickly assured me it was the best part of their week. But most telling, when friends and relatives visited from out of town, they always made the winery their first stop, showing them around as if they owned the place. It was entertaining to sit back and watch them deliver well-versed spiels on the operations of the winery, sending me an occasional conspiratorial wink.

The take these octogenarians shared on the situation seemed to be one of acceptance, served with a scoop of optimism. They had lived through a few wars and a Great Depression, after all. As I told them of our immediate plans, they talked up the move as an adventure to be enjoyed, a tabula rasa to be envied. They confided that some of the worst events in their long lives had evolved into their greatest opportunities, providing touching stories that backed up these claims. There was no mention of "when one door closes," etcetera—they were too savvy to reduce it to platitudes—and their sentiments resonated as I listened. All in all, I thought I held up pretty well. I'm not sure if it was because of the antidepressants I was taking or because of their splendid attitude, but I felt much better after spending my last shift with them. I was a little more grounded, better equipped to handle the coming changes. Wisdom: It is, indeed, all it's cracked up to be.

After the last customer left, Roberta, Flo, Shirley, and I sat down at the table for the last time with glasses of iced tea, sitting in our soiled damp aprons. The heat emanated from the nearby wall unit as I divided our tips from the blue and white tea pot; it held over three hundred dollars that day. Out of habit, Shirley took a paper towel from her apron pocket and rubbed at some blemish on the table. Roberta crossed her hands and sat looking at them, perfectly still. Flo passed a white saucer with slices of fresh lemon to me. There wasn't the usual light conversation; in fact, there was no conversation at all for a while. None of us wanted this.

After an uncomfortable silence, Roberta suddenly smiled and said she might "just get on that old Greyhound and come to Colorado" to see us some day. Her son was a driver for Greyhound Bus Company in Milwaukee, and she loved "ridin' that dog." I sure hoped that was true. But in fact, that was the last time I ever saw Roberta, as she passed away some years later. We rarely made it back to the Delta after we left, although I did remember to call every December 21 on her birthday. She always laughed when she heard my voice, saying, "I just knew you were going to call me today!"

Everyone sitting around the table in the overheated dining room that afternoon knew that Roberta was just trying to perk us up. She had been our head cheerleader since early May, after all. None of the rest of us had much to say, though. We were lost in our thoughts as we sat together for the last time, the ceiling fan spinning slowly above us. Finally, we all agreed that it had been a hell of a ride and raised our glasses in a toast, eyes moist.

Roberta and Flo slowly began packing up the pottery and the blackened pots and pans, while Shirley and I cleaned the dining rooms and removed the framed lace from the tea room walls. Half the stuff I gave away; the other half was headed to McCarty's. The newsprint informing everyone of our closing had barely dried before the idea of reopening the tea room on the McCarty compound in Merigold surfaced. They weren't buying the business—the only thing of value we had to offer was our reputation—but we were very pleased with the knowledge that Roberta and Flo would continue their jobs at the new venue. According to the *Commercial Appeal* in Memphis, Tennessee (Thomas, December 1990):

> "We're going to run the tea room with the same help, the same dishes, and the same four cracked glasses," said McCarty, whose pottery is prized across the country. "The tea room has been very successful, and the area needs it. Everyone is appalled that Sam and Diane are leaving, but they can't live this way."

The McCartys paid us well for the tables, chairs, and other restaurant paraphernalia we had accumulated. We nobly threw in the large stacks of pottery they had so generously donated nearly a decade earlier. "The Gallery" tea room was scheduled to open the following spring.

At the winery next door, the young man who had replaced Ray was busy talking to the last timers as they streamed through the tasting room, reminiscing about their time spent there. He choked up a few times too, I learned later. James had enjoyed his six months or so at the winery and had already carved a big place in the hearts of those with whom he worked. The college boys who had worked the vineyard and bottling line packed up the remains of the warehouse as Sam hosed down the cellar for the last time. One student, Collier Parker, was an art major at Delta State. Just before he left for the last time, he gave us a beautiful painting of the Sunflower River. Unbeknown to us, he had painted it a couple of weeks before from the bridge on our place, so that we could take a piece of the farm with us to Colorado. Today the large canvas depicting our beautiful river hangs in the most prominent spot in our living room.

It was a tough day for everyone. We didn't get over it, but we did get through it.

Leaving the tea room at dusk, I got into my car and drove halfway up the winding road between the winery and the house. I stopped the car, got out, and leaned on the hood to watch the spectacular sunset to the west. Across the bayou, I noticed Jack driving the little red tractor on one of the turn rows in the vineyard. Suddenly, he stopped, climbed down, took his hat off, and also looked west. He seemed unaware of my presence on the road.

The late afternoon was cold and quiet. I studied the bare limbs of the cypress trees in the bayou, their smooth gray trunks emerging from the still water. I inhaled the sweet smoke drifting down from the large fireplace in our home. I could hear some creature, probably a beaver, splashing near the banks below. The completion of my last day at the winery and tea room, it appeared, would be magnificent.

A moment later, just as the sun ducked behind the endless Delta horizon, Jack happened to look my way. We studied each other for a long minute. He placed his hat over his heart and lifted his other hand into the air, slowly waving his arm back and forth a few times. Deeply moved, I responded in kind. We looked at each other across the untamed bayou for a minute longer. Then I got back into my car and drove the rest of the way home.

CHAPTER 24

An Offer We Could Refuse

December 1990
Clarion-Ledger
Jackson, Mississippi
Court system gets blame for Merigold winery closing
By Dan Davis

. . . The Rushings felt that the evidence and the concessions by the fired employee's attorneys were enough to get a conviction. But this jury, he said, apparently didn't understand what was happening. Now the Rushings are closing the winery and pulling up stakes. Their next stop is Colorado.

And Rushing is carrying with him anger at the judicial system that he feels let him down. It's a little ironic that Mississippi has trouble luring and retaining businesses because of the state's education system, its poorly prepared workforce and its bloody past. Now a breakdown in the judicial system is being blamed for the loss of one of the state's homegrown and pioneering businesses.

The most surprising reaction to news of our leaving came in the form of a phone call on Christmas Eve, just after the kids had gone to bed.

"Mr. Rushing," the man began in a lazy Southern drawl. "You probably don't know me, but I live right across the (Mississippi)

River. Right outside-a Lake Village. I farm a few grapes over here and make a little wine, time to time."

"What can I do for you?" Sam asked, after the man identified himself. Everyone in the Delta knew the name but we didn't know him personally.

"Well, I been talking to some folks over here and we just don't think it's right that y'all are being forced outta your home like this."

"Well, thank you, Sir, but we don't feel like we have much choice," Sam replied tersely. We were both weary of this debate. It seemed everywhere we went, someone was trying to talk us out of leaving.

"Well, I appreciate that and everything but it don't have to end like this, ya know." He coughed a deep smoker's cough and continued. "I guess what I'm sayin' is, me and my buddies can take care of that Russell clan. You just say the word."

That certainly got Sam's attention.

"Not sure what you're saying here," he said, looking at me with a bewildered expression.

Curious, I got off the couch and made my way over to Sam, leaning closely to listen in. We could hear "Silent Night" playing in the background over the phone.

"Well-sir," he said. "I guess what I mean is this." He paused for a moment. "Some people just need killin'."

"Wait," Sam said. "What are you talking about?"

"Well-sir, nobody oughta have to put up with trash like 'at," he said. "We can take care of the whole bunch and ain't nobody gonna know a Gol-darn thing about who done it." He went on to say that he had trustworthy friends lined up and a sound plan in place. We got the impression he was sort of looking forward to it.

Astounded, Sam firmly told the man that would not be helpful. There was a bit more back and forth, but Sam finally convinced him to give up his plan. I was standing next to him as he hung up the phone.

"Was that what I think it was?" I asked. "An offer for a hit?"

"Sure was," Sam said. We looked at each other for a moment and then burst out laughing. I guess we were in sore need of comic relief at that point, and this otherworldly proposal provided it. When he told me the name, I recognized it as a large, wealthy family that was notoriously "connected," as they say. We talked a while longer as we finished our glasses of wine. Sam poked the dying fire as I stuffed the Christmas stockings hanging from the antique mantel that had once graced my grandmother's house. Checking the doors, Sam headed off to bed.

I sat down in my favorite chair and looked around the family room, colorful holiday decorations interspersed with moving boxes. The lighted Christmas tree stood tall, adorned with handmade ornaments, some of which dated back to our own childhoods in the fifties. The only sounds were the crackling fire and soft music playing seasonal favorites on the radio. The brightly wrapped gifts from friends and family seemed dwarfed by boxes marked "Lizzie's Toys" and "Bathroom Towels." Like a child, I wondered what was in the beautifully wrapped packages. Such a strange juxtaposition, I thought, of the known and the unknown, much like the future of my family.

As I sat there alone, I pondered how the Rushing family had gotten to such a place in life that we were asking a hit man to stand down on Christmas Eve. I thought about "that Russell clan," as he had called them, and wondered about Ray's family. I had heard through the grapevine that his sister had given birth to a baby boy in June, just a month after the break-in. I heard they had named him Kenneth. I knew it was a dangerous time to bring a new child into the family, and I hoped no harm would come to her and the baby in the wake of all that had happened.

It is often said that truth is stranger than fiction, and that is a fact. Ray's baby nephew, born just a few weeks after the Sunflower River ran red, would grow up to be a major player in the conclusion of this story three decades later. He, too, would become a victim of Ray's perverse sense of entitlement. This time, however, Ray would go too far. This time, lives would be lost.

I was greatly saddened by the exchange Sam had been forced to engage in on our last Christmas Eve in our beautiful home. Its ugliness had shaken me to the core. Yet, as I sat there on that cold night, I knew that some deep, dark part of me was grateful that someone had made the grim offer. I'm not proud of it, but there it is.

The next few days passed slowly and quickly. On Christmas morning, the children opened their gifts only to put them right back into a box to go onto the truck. I packed up the house, making bizarre decisions in the process. I tucked the long-forgotten stuffed frog from the back of Matt's closet into his box and accidentally threw away his well-loved Mr. Rabbit. I mindlessly loaded boxes of clothes that Lizzie had outgrown two years earlier into the trunk of my car. I carefully packed the cheap plastic patio table in bubble wrap and left behind the antique cherry dresser my grandmother had willed me. When I was unloading boxes a few weeks later in Colorado, I found a can of pork and beans and a harmonica in my underwear box.

The day before we left, Lizzie and I drove out to Liv's farm to say goodbye to her. She was waiting for us at the door in her worn beige stocking cap and blue work jumper. The day was cold, but her house was oppressively hot. We quietly made our way past her husband, who was lying on a cot in the living room, all bundled up and dangerously close to the open gas heater. He was very old and had been bedridden for years. Lizzie and I sat with Liv at her kitchen table, holding hands and trying to pretend that this was just another routine visit. But of course, we knew it wasn't. It was the end of a lifelong, love-filled relationship that could never be duplicated. I watched as Liv's old black hand gently kneaded Lizzie's tiny white one and was nearly overcome with sorrow.

"Everything's gonna be all right, Baby Girl," she said, over and over. I still don't know if she was talking to me or Lizzie. Both, I suspect. The three of us made promises we knew we couldn't keep as we hugged each other for the last time and made our way towards the door. Lizzie waved goodbye from the backseat as we pulled out of the muddy driveway and onto the main road leading to Mound Bayou.

Liv died a few years after we left. We never got the chance to see her beautiful face again. According to her granddaughter, some of her last words were about us. She said Liv was waiting on me to "bring the children by" the day she died. This is all I am able to say about this.

Unlike me, Sam had planned his part of the exodus well. He had borrowed the trailer his brother-in-law used for his race car and rented the largest U-Haul available. Sam's cousin Sara and her husband, Vance, had agreed to pull it as they accompanied us on the three-day trek to Colorado. My brother was assigned the arduous task of driving cross-country with two young children and me in my Ford Taurus. Sam was bringing up the rear of the convoy in his pickup truck, pulling the long trailer.

Fortunately, we had found a man from Merigold to rent our house starting January first, which would help pay for the mountain of expenses to come. He promised to keep an eye on the winery, and I recall wondering if he realized what he had signed on for. I was glad he wasn't bringing a young family with him. Jack agreed to check on the place as well, as we handed him the keys to the tractor, the winery, and the tea room. Folks from all over the Delta brought food to get us through the tough days ahead as we packed up our lives. A dear friend made up a large basket of homemade cookies and snacks for the long trip to Colorado. Another offered to clean the house after we left. We hadn't been to our cabin in the woods since before the trial, and I tried to remember what we were leaving behind. All I could think of was a bent red colander.

When, on the last day, we realized that we couldn't fit anything else into the trucks, Sam said, "That's it. No more room." I looked around at the stray furniture and unmarked boxes on the front porch and wondered what was in them. More boxes and furniture remained in the house. I had no clear idea what we were taking and what was still sitting there, exposed to the December weather. But I agreed it was time to go. I called and asked Roberta to sell whatever was left and keep the profits. I sorely missed some of these things later, but the important parcels, Lizzie and Matt, were safely strapped in the back seat as we pulled away from our house for the last time.

Our home of fourteen years looked as though it had been evacuated during a natural disaster. There were abandoned bikes in the front yard and a lonely swing set in the back. Sam's muddy three-wheeler was parked near the sidewalk where he had left it a month earlier. Sassy's green doghouse sat on the front porch, its pink floral bedding half in and half out. The winery and tea room grounds appeared equally dismal as we drove by. The flowerbeds had been shamefully neglected, and it seemed to me that the dead marigolds were turned toward us, begging us to stay. A few empty wine boxes flapped in the cold wind near the crushing pad. Jack's red tractor was parked askew on the concrete behind the warehouse. I looked up at the sign painted above, "The Winery Rushing—Bonded Winery Mississippi Number One." A dozen or so friends nodded and waved as we passed through the parking lot, processing the finality of this somber caravan of trucks and trailers.

As we pulled onto the road, I looked to the east to see if Ray had shown up to witness his final conquest personally. I sighed with relief as I saw no sign of his old green car. We were still reeling from his most recent threats, and Sam had seen Emmitt driving slowly past the turnoff a few times the week before. We were sure they had caught wind of our plans to leave and were congratulating themselves for running us out of our home. The thought sickened me. That said, by then I had begun to look at our departure as a pyrrhic victory of sorts, escaping, as we were, in one piece.

Less than an hour later, we approached the mighty Mississippi at the Greenville Bridge, nearly two miles long. Behind us, row after row of desiccated cotton plants faded from view, their tattered white fibers blowing in the wind. I peered over the railing at the swirling brown water below, watching a tow boat slowly maneuver its way around the bridge pilings. Just ahead I saw Sara and Vance carefully driving their white truck pulling some of our most treasured belongings. Behind I saw the silhouette of Sam, alone, hauling the rest. I exhaled a deep breath as we crossed the sign on the bridge that welcomed us—Arkansas, the Natural State. I took one last look at the river as our humming tires left the aging bridge and touched land once again with a hard bump and a loud thump. The pavement became smooth again and the high-pitched noise immediately subsided.

I smiled at my brother sitting beside me on the front seat, grateful for this tangible harbinger of better things to come. Ray and his father were behind us. All that we owned was with us. Uncertainty was ahead of us. But my family was safe. I looked in the rearview mirror one last time, the darkness of the past nine months receding in the distance as quickly as the huge metal bridge towering over the Mississippi River. I closed my eyes and mumbled a word of thanks. I felt as though we had outrun the Devil himself.

CHAPTER 25

Di Has a Violent Streak

December 13, 1990
Delta Democrat Times
Greenville, Mississippi
Rushings shutting down Merigold operation, moving to Colorado
By Sonya Kimbrell

. . . They have friends where they're going and they've already found a house though neither has a job lined up.

She (Di) said opening another tea room is a possibility but they have no plans to try to start another winery. She said she hopes marketing gourmet foods will be possible.

"We want to work for the other guy for a while," she said.

. . . She said she doesn't understand why the situation had to turn out like it has. But, in the end everything will work out for the best, although it's hard to guess what's in the future for them.

Traveling with Lizzie and Matt was no small feat; those were the days when they drew a line between themselves in the backseat and dared each other to cross it. There were no such things as iPads back then; license plate games and whatever was on the radio or the tape player was all we had to offer. My mother had donated a few books on tape for the trip. Her favorites were of the Western genre, and I thought those might be entertaining for the four of us as we drove twelve hundred miles west to our new home. I chose one that was set in Colorado to give us a little something to look forward to. The reader's voice was deep and gravelly as he told the tale of a lonely sheriff in a dusty cow town. The kids seemed intrigued by the simple plot, munching chocolate chip cookies and sipping water in the backseat as they listened to the story. Around Oklahoma City, however, the narrative suddenly transitioned into a mildly lurid sex scene. "The strong woman standing before him suddenly looked like a little girl who needed a spanking, and he was just the sheriff to give it to her. He looked at her flushed face, his eyes drifting to her plump bosom below. He cupped her breast in his large hand as Maria raised her chin in defiance."

"Whoa," I said, frantically searching for the Stop button. "I don't think y'all need to hear this." I quickly pulled the tape from the player and put it back into the box.

"Mama, no," Lizzie whined. "This is the best part!" Matt nodded at me, in firm solidarity with his sister. At wit's end, I nearly gave in to the little ingrates. Then I thought, "Damn it, this is one thing I can control!" Ignoring their protests, I pushed another tape into the player amid loud protests. My big brother wasn't much support as he continued to drive, an annoying grin on his face. Apparently, he had been amused by the scurrilous dialog and the contest of wills that followed. Disgusted by all three of them, I rode in silence for a while. After a few miles, I lightened up a bit and reclined the seat, finally appreciating how beautifully normal the whole exchange had been.

Three days later, we pulled out of the hotel parking lot in Cortez, Colorado. It was December 30, 1990, Lizzie's ninth birthday. She had been sick all night, vomiting every hour or so. The weather was atrocious that morning, the wind blowing so hard that the snow seemed to fall horizontally. The heater worked hard to counter the frigid temperature outside, and the windshield wipers proved woefully inadequate. I watched the dangerous sway of Sam's trailer in front of us as we passed a sign that read, "Norwood - 110 Miles." Our caravan slowly navigated its way north through the remote Canyons of the Ancients as the blizzard grew stronger. The old Christmas hymn, "In the Bleak Midwinter," looped over and over in my mind as we passed through desolate snow-covered reservations unique to the Southwest. My car, whose stomping grounds had been the flatlands of the Mississippi Delta, was ill-equipped to grip the slick road that wound its way over the pass to our new home. Every time we slid on the black ice, I was thrown into a terrified panic, screaming expletives at my brother and scaring the hell out of my children. By the time we got to Norwood, everyone in the car was pale with exhaustion and fright.

Our new home was situated about three miles west of town in a subdivision of sorts. Like many in Colorado, the neighborhood was a mix of new and old, large and small, nice and, well, not-so-nice. The house we had rented, sight unseen, was just fine, however. It was small to be sure, and a bit dark for my taste, but it was a welcome sight as we pulled into the driveway. We unlocked the door and went inside. On the kitchen counter sat a gigantic floral arrangement that had arrived that morning. I guess the realtor had arranged for the florist to come in earlier in the day. The tiny card clipped on the green plastic spike read, "Welcome to your new home. We miss you already." It was from a friend in Cleveland. Words cannot express how much that beautiful bouquet of winter blooms lifted our spirits as we unloaded sheets for the beds and food for our dinner that night.

The snowstorm continued through the night and all the next day. I waited for it to let up enough for me to go to the grocery store, but by three o'clock, it was obvious that the white-out was there to stay. Having lived on potato chips, apple juice, and peanut butter sandwiches for three days, we were all ready for some real food, and we had none. I bundled up in my hat, coat and gloves and headed towards town. Within a mile, my car was stuck in a shallow ditch by the road, headlights faintly visible in a bank of snow. This proved to be just the first of many times I found myself off the road in the coming months. Luckily, a CDOT driver happened by within minutes. He graciously pulled me out and sent me on my way.

I crept the last mile into Norwood at the pace of a three-toed sloth, finally arriving at the only market in town. The small lot sat under a foot of snow, and two large lumps of white were parked near the door. Grateful to have arrived, I slipped and slid my way to the door in my navy blue Ferragamos. Pushing the door to no avail, I looked up to see the sign hanging on the inside.

Closing at 3:00 today—Happy New Year!

I had totally forgotten that it was New Year's Eve.

That night we had cheese and crackers for dinner and Rollos for dessert. Sara and Vance had picked up some beer when they stopped for gas, and we had half a bottle of apple juice for the kids. I found two bottles of wine in a box marked "Kitchen Stuff," and the party was on. The storm outside continued to rage as the seven of us sat inside, cozy and welcoming in the new year. After Sara and the kids went to bed, Sam, Nelson, and Vance continued the celebration with wine, beer, and an increasingly unhealthy sense of adventure. I listened to their banter as I began tidying up the kitchen a bit.

At around ten o'clock, Sam had a brilliant idea.

"Hey, let's go check out Norwood Hill," he said. "I heard it is really something." I froze at the words. Even I knew how treacherous Norwood Hill was, with vertical plunges to over a thousand feet below. I had read about this unforgiving stretch of highway in a brochure a few years before when we were skiing in Telluride. The frigid wind howled outside as his dangerous plan quickly progressed.

"Sounds good," Vance said, setting aside his glass of wine and reaching for his coat. Nelson offered to drive as he grabbed the keys from the kitchen counter and headed toward the back door.

"Like hell y'all are going out there," I said, in a low, dangerous voice, slowly turning from the sink and stepping towards Sam. The anger simmering from me was palpable as I stood ramrod straight before him, my face just inches from his.

"I did not abandon my beautiful life in Mississippi and come to this . . . this frozen wasteland just to see you get killed on our first night," I said, shaking with rage. "You are going exactly nowhere tonight."

Turning around, I held out my hand and instructed my brother, "Nelson, give me those damned keys." He stood there silently, unsure what to do, looking at me, then Sam, then back at me.

"Now!" I shouted.

"Come on, Di," Sam pleaded. "Don't be like that. We'll be fine."

I looked my husband straight in the eye, made a hard fist, pulled my right arm back as far as I could, and punched him in the nose. Blood trickled down to his lip as we looked at each other, both shocked by this violent streak that had remained dormant for the first thirty-seven years of my life.

"You hit me . . ." Sam said, no sign of anger in his voice, just astonishment. He backed over to the kitchen table and slowly sat down on the nearest chair. He looked up at me in awe, gingerly holding his handkerchief to his bloody nose, cautiously studying my next move.

The rest of us stood in the poorly lit kitchen surrounded by moving boxes, the crusts of PB and Js sitting on paper plates, and beer cans. Vance and Nelson nervously looked at each other and then at their shoes. No one knew what to say. Finally, Nelson quietly took the keys from his pocket and passed them over to me.

"Thank you," I muttered, summoning as much dignity as I could. I put my wine glass in the sink and headed towards the bedroom. "Happy New Year," I said over my shoulder as I continued down the narrow hallway. I was embarrassed, but sort of proud of myself at the same time. After all, I reasoned, I had just saved three lives.

Five minutes later, I heard Sam rummaging through the unpacked box in the bathroom. Then he entered the bedroom and lay beside me on the bed, fully clothed. I lay beside him for a few minutes, my anger slowly dissipating with exhaustion. Finally, I rolled over and peered at him in the darkness. His eyes were closed and he seemed to be asleep. Leaning closer, I saw that he had stuffed one of my tampons up his left nostril.

The next day brought sunshine and with it, better moods. Lizzie and Matt got up, ate breakfast, and ran outside to build their first snowman. I gave them a red scarf to wrap around its neck. Later that morning, two little girls suddenly appeared at the end of our short driveway. Standing side by side, they looked to be about the same age as my two. They both had wavy brown hair hanging down to their shoulders. The smaller one was dressed from head to toe in hot pink and had mittens hanging on strings from the sleeves of her coat. The way they stood there perfectly still, quietly staring, reminded me of the two little girls at the end of the hotel corridor in *The Shining.* I decided that if they said, "Come and play with us," I was going to pack up and go back home.

"Hi," the younger one said to Matt. "What's your name?"

"Matt," he said hesitantly, then looked at me to rescue him. He wasn't sure if he wanted to pursue this relationship.

"What grade are you in?" she asked.

"First," he replied.

"Me too," she said. She paused a moment. "We already have a Matt in first grade." Then the two little girls turned in unison and crossed the street back to their house. Matt looked at me, shrugged his shoulders, and went back to work on the snowman.

The next day, I loaded up the kids and we scouted the town looking for the school, the post office, and other places of interest. The school, located a block over from the highway running through town, looked friendly. It housed grades Pre-K–12. The playground featured equipment ranging from a tiny green playhouse to a regulation basketball court. Apparently, their mascot was the Mavericks, which suited this ranching community well.

Norwood was situated on top of Wright's Mesa at about 7,000 feet, so the town itself was flat. But the views around it were spectacular, as it was surrounded by tall mountains, the most iconic being Lone Cone. I noticed that there didn't appear to be much tourism here, however. We still weren't sure what we were going to do, but Sam was hoping to pursue his new love of glassblowing, which required a steady flow of visitors to survive. The houses were modest but well-kept, and the few businesses that lined the main street seemed to be filled with patrons. At the post office, I saw a notice about the school's beginning again the next Monday. I knew it would be a hard day all around, especially for Lizzie and Matt.

The following afternoon, we drove thirty minutes to Telluride and met some friends from the Delta. Every year, a dozen or so faculty members from Delta State and their friends came to ski during the Christmas holidays. I recall how strange I felt as we sat by the hot tub at their luxurious hotel. A month before, I would have fit right in, but that evening I felt like an outsider as these old friends soaked, laughed, and talked about their beautiful day on the mountain. I was already sensing that Thomas Wolfe was right—you can't go home again.

Monday, January 7, was the first day of school after the holidays. Lizzie deliberated for an hour the night before over what she should wear, finally deciding to go with her default pink everything. Matt carefully packed his Teenage Mutant Ninja Turtles backpack with pencils and paper. He pondered putting one of his TMNT action figures in but decided against it at the last minute. They were well-versed in what was cool in Mississippi, but they had no idea what was *de rigueur* in Colorado. They were such little troopers.

I was as nervous as the kids when we pulled up in front of the school. Great banks of snow had been plowed to the edge in a circle of sorts. I felt as though I were parking in a big ole pie crust. Children aged four to eighteen poured out of buses and cars in the parking lot. Everyone seemed to be wearing Wranglers and plaid shirts, even the girls. "Colorado," I muttered, "Where the men are men and the women are too." Scores of cowboy boots and hats added to the strange array of apparel. It was as different as could be from our small elementary school in the Delta, where one didn't go to school unless one's shoes were highly polished.

We entered the building and immediately came upon the office where we needed to register. The secretary welcomed us warmly and handed me some forms to fill out. Lizzie and Matt sat next to me, wide-eyed and anxious as I recorded their names, birthdates, and other pertinent information. As I handed in the forms, she asked Matt if he liked Colorado so far.

"Yes, Ma'am," he replied. She was surprised by his response and congratulated him on his fine manners, unaware that it wasn't much of an anomaly where we came from. Nor was it much of a choice. Then she leaned over and asked Lizzie what brought us to Colorado. Her earnest reply made me want to crawl under the copy machine beside me and hide behind the boxes of paper.

"There was a bad man after us," she said matter-of-factly, pushing her pink glasses up with her index finger.

The secretary slowly straightened and looked at me. I could just imagine what she thought; I'm sure it was something along the lines of, "They must be running from the law." There we stood, I with my big hair, dressed as though I were going to Sunday School, and my two little refugee children, running from some nefarious presence in Mississippi. I didn't know what to say, so I just looked at her as though this were a perfectly sane reason to show up over a thousand miles from home in the middle of the school year.

We followed the secretary down the long hall. The kids walked slowly, staring into the classrooms as we passed by. I knew it was as terrifying for my children to be "the new kid" as it has been for all children since the beginning of time. First, we took Lizzie to her classroom. The little girl in Lizzie's class who lived across the street was especially nice, greeting her as though they were good friends. She took her arm and showed her to her new desk. After a quick goodbye, we headed a few doors down to the first-grade classroom. Matt tried to hide behind me as we entered. The teacher smiled warmly as she introduced him. He was quickly approached by the other Matt in his class, and they seemed to hit it off immediately. They remained good friends until the end of the year, often enjoying play dates after school. He lived on a beautiful ranch west of town, with horses and scores of other large farm animals. I guess there was room in the first grade for two Matts, after all.

The next day dawned cold and snowy, and the wind was unbelievably strong. I soon learned that this was the norm in Norwood, winter and summer. This would be the first time the kids had ever ridden on a school bus, and while the idea was heady for them, it was nerve-racking for me. I imagined them awkwardly walking down the aisle looking for a seat and being rejected, just like Forrest Gump was a few years later. The four of us walked against the powerful wind toward the little lean-to that served as a bus stop. We sat together quietly on the ice-encrusted bench until the bus came; then Sam and I made our way back to the house.

I spent most of that day looking out the window at the bus stop, watching the snow blast horizontally across Wright's Mesa in powerful bursts. Deer wandered through the field behind our house, looking for something to eat. The kids' snowman had lost the pine branch that had served as his left arm. His red scarf had likely blown to Telluride by then. He looked cold, desolated in a desolate landscape.

It was a good week for the kids, however. They quickly made friends and the teacher soon learned that they were very smart. They had both scored in the 98th percentile on their national standardized test earlier that year. I hoped that this would improve the less-than-stellar first impression we had made. On Friday, I went to the school around three o'clock to hand in their vaccination records and pick them up from school. As I waited to speak with the secretary, I overheard a conversation between two teachers.

"I have to take off next Tuesday," one was saying. "I have a doctor's appointment in Montrose, but they can't find a sub." This was a dilemma that seemed foreign to me at the time, but one I would become very familiar with in the coming years.

"I know," the other one said. "We have a real shortage of subs this year."

The conversation didn't register with me until I was chatting with the secretary a few minutes later. She seemed to be nicely recovered from the disturbing confession my nine-year old had made earlier in the week. She asked how the kids liked school and I assured her they were quite happy. Before leaving, I asked her, "Do y'all need a sub, by any chance? I think I have a teaching certificate from Mississippi."

"God, yes!" she replied, then paused. "But what do you mean, you 'think' you have one?"

"Well, I used to," I said, trying to remember where I had packed that damned piece of paper and feeling like a complete fool. This lady really did a number on my self-confidence. I soldiered on, however. "I mean, I did get a teaching degree. In 1976. From Mississippi State University." I paused and waited for her response. Crickets. "Because my Daddy insisted," I lamely added. Jesus, what was wrong with me?

The secretary was admirably unflappable. That, or she was desperate for subs—take your pick.

"Well, to answer your question, we would love for you to sub for us when you can," she said. "Our only requirements for subs are a teaching certificate and," she stopped and looked at me over the top of her reading glasses, "a background check." She was clearly gauging my reaction to that one.

I quickly assured her that wouldn't be a problem. Then I gathered the kids and headed home. TGIF.

CHAPTER 26

There's No Place Like Home

Obscurity brings safety.

—AESOP

The following week, Sam and Nelson headed back to Mississippi to return the trailer and wrap up some loose ends at the winery. It was going to be a sad trip for Sam, as he had been directed by the Feds at the Division of Alcohol, Tobacco and Firearms to "dispose" of the new wine that was still sitting in the tanks in the cellar. Because we had officially closed, we were forced to forfeit our Bonded Winery Mississippi Number One license to produce and sell wine. For the second time in a year, our beautiful wine would be trickling down the drain and into the Sunflower River, this time by Sam's own hand. The requirement was heartbreaking, but the law was clear.

I handed my husband and my brother a thermos of coffee and a partially eaten box of Vanilla Wafers, waving goodbye as they pulled onto the snowy road. As they drove away, the empty trailer rattled loudly behind them. I felt impossibly alone. Lizzie and Matt had left for school an hour earlier, so I had the dark little house to myself for the first time. I sensed another onslaught of self-indulgence coming, so I shook my head hard and told myself to get over it—I still had many boxes to unpack. We didn't know how long we would stay in Norwood, but we knew it would be at least until May, when school was out.

I poured myself another cup of coffee and began unpacking some dishes, setting them on the bottom shelf of the kitchen cabinet. I studied the intricate painting on one of the cups. It seemed much too fine for this place. I emptied the box, stuffed the newspaper back inside, and looked for a knife to open the next. In the drawer, I found a bundle of letters our friends and customers had sent before we left, tied in green yarn. Many of them remained unopened, having been received during the chaos of closing the business and packing up our lives. I sat on the floor of the kitchen, untied the string, and began reading. A few letters later, I went to the medicine cabinet to get another red pill, another antidepressant that had been prescribed to get me through the rough days in December. Just one more, I thought. The bottle that should have lasted another month was empty. That was when I knew I might have a problem.

Nothing exacerbates depression more than knowing you are depressed. This is especially true when you know you should be feeling grateful instead. I repeatedly told myself that the battle with Ray was finally over, that I should be overjoyed that our little family had escaped before anything else happened. And I was, of course. I knew we were fortunate to have been able to relocate to such a beautiful, safe place; that was a "good" thing. At the same time, however, I had lost my home, my tea room, and daily contact with my family and friends, and that was a "bad" thing. I couldn't seem to work through this train wreck in my head.

I had struggled with this dichotomy of emotions once before, the impossibly irreconcilable spikes of simultaneous joy and anguish. That time it had been much more devastating. The morning Lizzie was born, her twin brother, Claiborne, was stillborn. Five months before, Sam and I had been elated upon learning that we were having twins, but we also knew that the risk had just risen exponentially. Before I became pregnant, I weighed about 105 pounds, and I carried them both to term. When she was born, Lizzie weighed seven and a half pounds. The doctor told me a few days later that Claiborne had been about the same size.

The best thing that had ever happened to us and the worst thing that had ever happened came crashing down at the exact same moment in the early hours of December 30, 1981. In the months after, I vacillated between euphoria over my beautiful new daughter and deep sorrow over the son I would never know. I couldn't eat and I couldn't sleep. The only food that appealed to me was Liv's green beans; everything else tasted like chalk. Sam wept as he took down the other Jenny Lind crib soon after Lizzie and I got home from the hospital. Nursing Lizzie in my old rocking chair some nights, I swore I could hear Claiborne crying in the next room. On a few occasions, I got up to see where the cry was coming from. I rarely put my baby down, and Lizzie became my sole *raison d'etre*. This unhealthy state continued for a year or so, although it got better with time. It wasn't until Matt was born two and a half years later, however, that either of us felt normal again. The moment we heard his loud wail in the delivery room, most of the malaise lifted. Lizzie's birthday is still tough on Sam and me, though. We should be blowing out twice as many candles.

The cold, windy days in Norwood continued. I felt as though I were an automaton, getting the kids ready for school, watching them trudge through the snow to the bus stop, waiting for them to come home, and fixing them dinner at night. I was successful in getting off the antidepressants but remained dependent on the sleeping pills that provided a respite from my thoughts each night. I have great gaps in memory of those days, truth be told. Lizzie told me not too long ago that when she thinks of Norwood, she automatically thinks of badly burnt cinnamon toast. She said most days I went through half a loaf of bread before I could come up with two edible pieces.

Two weeks after he left, Sam was back from Mississippi, but he was already planning another important trip in early March to meet with some of our wassail customers and cookbook vendors. The cookbooks were continuing to sell at a rapid pace in the South, which I interpreted as proof that I still mattered to some people, somewhere. As pathetic as that sounds, I guess I was right; within a year, all six thousand copies had sold. I envied Sam and his next sojourn back to the familiarity of our old life. I wanted to go with him. I missed Mississippi.

As the snow continued, I began subbing at the high school, which helped both emotionally and financially. I had never taught before, and I had no idea if I would be good at it or not. At first, I struggled as I tried to be someone I wasn't—a strict, controlling substitute teacher. I thought that was what they were supposed to look like. Soon, however, I lightened up and started enjoying my new job immensely. I decided that the best tools I could bring to the classroom were a good sense of humor and a determination not to take myself too seriously. I told myself that anything I said or did was not likely to affect these teenagers much, one way or the other. This epiphany proved to be both accurate and vindicating.

I loved the school in Norwood. The students and teachers were warm and friendly, going to great lengths to include me in their busy lives. One of the students invited me to a small rodeo that spring. I laughed as I saw a baby girl with a big pink cowboy hat perched on her tiny head. Embroidered on the front were the words, "This IS my first rodeo!" My journey in learning the ranching vernacular was arduous at times, however. Coming from what seemed like another planet, I couldn't relate to the chatter of rodeos, sick heifers, and riding fences. That last one, *riding fences*, puzzled me for a week or more.

I was subbing for the high school P.E. teacher in the gym one day, my least favorite assignment as it required exercise, shouting, and ill-fitting clothing with an orange whistle as the only accessory. I had been called to supervise the boys' basketball team's scrimmage, their last warm-up before that night's game against their greatest rival, Telluride. As the period came to a close, I realized I had enjoyed the time spent with these sweet boys, and I was feeling a little athletic myself. I had actually made a basket during class, much to everyone's surprise, and the loud cheers that followed had been extremely gratifying. Emboldened, I decided to ask them about something that had been bothering me. Sitting on the bottom bleacher, I watched as they finished up and began shooting the basketballs into the large net container by the door.

"Can one of you please tell me what a fence is?" I shouted.

"A fence?" one of them asked. They all stopped shooting. Wiping their brows with the Maverick towels that hung from their sweat-pants, they looked at each other. Then at me. One of the seniors, basketball balanced between his hip and his right wrist, bravely stepped forward.

"Well, Mrs. Rushing," he began earnestly. The other boys looked at him and nodded, encouraging him to continue. They knew I was a bit strange, but they hadn't expected this. "A fence is a barrier we put around our pastures to keep the livestock in. You see, if you don't do that, then—"

I stopped him midsentence. I told him that I knew what fences were, of course. I just didn't understand how one could ride them. "Straddle them, perhaps," I muttered, drawing on the little dignity that remained.

The boys burst into laughter and in a rushed jumble of words, enlightened me on "riding fences." Deeply embarrassed, I decided not to tell them that I had thought a fence must have been some type of weird horse I had never heard of.

In March, Gertrude, the kids' godmother and my dear friend, flew in from the Delta to keep me company for a couple of weeks while Sam was away. Despite our age difference of nearly forty years, we had a lot in common. About a week after she arrived, Gertrude and I decided to drive to Montrose for groceries and supplies while Lizzie and Matt were in school. Montrose was about an hour and a half away, so we left as soon as their big yellow bus lumbered off. The trip was pleasant, as the weather was crystal clear and the scenery breathtaking. As we approached the intersection of Highway 62 and 550 at Ridgway, we looked to the right. Ten miles down the road sat Ouray, a small town known primarily for its hot springs. Although we had heard of it for years, Sam and I had never been there.

"Would you just look at that, Gertrude?" I said, my eyes scanning the valley floor. The snow sparkled like diamonds, surrounded by snow-capped mountains. Evergreens sagged with the weight of the heavy snowfall of the night before. I pulled the car over to the side for a moment and looked south. I was dazzled by the beauty. "That town has got to be gorgeous," I said.

"Let's go check it out," Gertrude suggested. Flipping my blinker up, I turned right onto the highway and headed south. The narrow road followed a winding valley along the Uncompahgre River, the Ute word for "red springs." Apparently, there were still a lot of minerals in them thar hills, and their sediment lent the river a rusty tint. The source was Lake Como, a beautiful spot high in the mountains just ahead. As the Uncompahgre made its way towards Ridgway, white steam rose from the hot springs that fed it, creating a dreamy, meandering trail. To the west, Mt. Sneffels, checking in at over fourteen thousand feet, loomed above as we made our way south to Ouray.

Fifteen minutes later, we reached the tiny town of nine hundred residents. The first thing we saw was the hot springs pool, which was divided into several sections, all held at different temperatures. Bathers sat in the steamy water, socializing and marveling, no doubt, at their good fortune. Further down, a tall berm of snow stood in the middle of Main Street, little paths carved out for pedestrians to cross the street. A few folks were out and about, dressed in bright snow gear and moving slowly. A huge truck was blocking the northbound lane as it unloaded boxes into the town's only market. The American flag blew happily in front of the post office.

Up the hill to the left, I saw the school, the most important building in town as far as I was concerned. We carefully drove up the steep slope towards the playground, which was full of small children playing on colorful playground equipment. They seemed happy, screaming loudly as they threw snowballs. A three-legged dog was trying to keep up with them, without much luck. I would learn later that she belonged to one of the teachers who lived down the street.

Her name was Tess, and she always came to play with the children as soon as she heard the recess bell. Her nickname was Tripod.

A sense of peace filled my soul as we drove about the little town. Victorian houses of all colors and sizes lined the hilly streets. There was a small ski hill at the south end of town which, according to the sign, was maintained by the Woman's Club of Ouray, founded in 1897. It featured a free tow lift, and I had no doubt that this place was the first stop for kids when the last school bell rang. At City Hall, a notice posted outside told us that admission to the hot springs pool was free for all children living in Ouray. Pondering this, we looked up and saw a frozen blue waterfall gracing the northeast side of the town.

Gertrude spotted a small pastry shop just across the street. We carefully made our way over the icy slope of Sixth Avenue. The tinkling of a bell over the door announced our arrival. Stepping inside, the intoxicating smell of fresh beignets enveloped us. New Orleans. The French Market. I felt as though we had just stepped into the Café Du Monde. Mr. Doyle, the owner, was sprinkling powdered sugar on the pastries as we walked up to the counter. His wife Evelyn poured us a cup of café au lait, rich with the scent of chicory. She asked us in her beautiful Louisiana accent where we would like to sit. Then she placed a small plate in the center of the table.

I think that day at La Papillon Bakery was a turning point for me. As I bit into a hot beignet, I was transformed back to the smells and tastes of home. Those pastries were like manna from heaven. Maybe, I thought, Thomas Wolfe was mistaken. Turns out I was wrong about the ski hill being the school kids' first stop each day, however. In the coming fall, I would learn that their first stop was this bakery, located just around the corner from the school. Every afternoon at 3:30, the owners of La Papillon put out a large tray of free, "day-old donuts" for the kids to dash by and grab. I don't think they were a day old though; some of them were suspiciously warm.

Although I didn't know it as Gertrude and I sipped our coffee that day, my young family would soon be spending a great deal of time in this little bakery. Our first glass shop in Ouray would be located right next door, and for a year, we would live in the small apartment just above it. With just one bedroom, Matt and Lizzie were relegated to a storage area with no windows and a six-foot ceiling. It was strangely situated between the two floors of the hundred-year-old building, with access down a ladder leading from the corner of our bedroom. With no room for two beds, we constructed makeshift bunkbeds, and the clearance on the upper bunk was about two feet. Despite this, the kids fought over the top bed, as kids everywhere do, I suppose. It was quite a departure from their fancy bedrooms in Merigold, but they loved it.

Just after we moved to Ouray a few months later, Lizzie began selling wildflower seeds in front of the shop, where she made a surprising profit. Soon, Matt was hired to sweep the floors of the Doyles' bakery for a dollar a day. Such lucrative employment was a big deal for a second grader, and he took his job seriously. One day he came racing over to our place with his new friend, Shane.

"Mama!" he said, "Come look at the donut tree! It's really cool!"

"It's a secret, though," Shane added in a whisper, putting his finger to his lips. His light blue eyes were huge behind the magnified lenses of his glasses.

I followed them out the front door of the shop and over to the small patch of grass behind La Papillon. Mr. Doyle stood there proudly in his white apron, a huge smile on his broad face and a cigarette in his right hand. He had stuck a large tree branch into the ground. Hanging from each branch was a white string with a single Cheerio dangling from it. The donut tree.

As Gertrude and I drove out of town and headed north towards Montrose, a child-like excitement gripped me. Finding Ouray had been nothing less than a spiritual experience for me. I knew with every fiber of my being that this was where we belonged. I couldn't wait to show Sam and the kids this hidden treasure I had found deep in a valley in the San Juan Mountains.

Four weeks later, my family pulled into Ouray. It was their first time seeing the town I had spoken of, nonstop, for weeks, and it was as spectacular as I had remembered. Once again, the sun glittered on the snowdrifts. Once again, happy people maneuvered the berms on Main Street, calling out to each other from across the street. My family was as captivated as I was, and I quipped that somehow, we seemed to have landed in the middle of a 1940s Frank Capra movie. We drove by the school, the ski hill, and the courthouse, built a hundred years earlier. Unknowingly, one of the houses we most admired, a small green Victorian built in 1879, would become ours just a year later, thanks to a VA loan Sam was able to secure.

The four of us pulled into a parking space in front of La Papillon. Mr. and Mrs. Doyle welcomed me warmly, remembering that I had grown up in the Mississippi Delta, not too far from their hometown of New Orleans. I introduced the rest of my family. The Doyles were delighted by the kids' "Ma'ams and Sirs," as it reminded them of their home in Cajun Country. Lizzie and Matt stuck their noses to the glass as they pointed and made their pastry selection.

"Here ya go, Sugar," Mrs. Doyle said as she handed Lizzie her warm doughnut, wrapped in white wax paper.

"Thank you, Ma'am," she replied. Mrs. Doyle came around the counter and hugged her, eyes shining brightly. Sam and I looked at each other and smiled. We were home.

CHAPTER 27

Bloom Where You Are Planted

September 17, 1992
Ouray County Plaindealer
Ouray, Colorado
Meet the New Ouray Teachers
By Sara Seloheim

*New Ouray English, journalism and eighth grade social studies
teacher Di Rushing is looking forward to the coming school year.*

"I'm excited about it," she says. "I think it is going to be great."

*. . . Rushing became an English teacher "because I have always
loved words. I am a fifth generation school teacher," she adds. . . .
They had traveled in this region on vacation and loved to ski at
Telluride. So in December 1990, they moved here.*

"The main consideration was for our two children," she adds.

*. . . She goes back to registering students for classes with a smile
on her face. Di Rushing is right at home.*

Just two months after visiting La Papillon, Sam began fulfilling the
dream that provided him flow by opening Ouray Glassworks. We
owned and operated that business for twenty-seven years before selling it to a beautiful young millennial named Annie. After subbing
for a year, I secured a position at Ouray High School, where I taught

English, journalism, and psychology for twenty years. I loved every minute of it. In 2014, I pulled the trigger and retired, just in time to welcome two new granddaughters, born nine days apart. Soon after, I began making pottery at the shop in the tradition of a wonderful couple named McCarty from Merigold, Mississippi.

Lizzie completed her undergraduate studies at the University of Colorado in Boulder, where she graduated Phi Beta Kappa and Magna Cum Laude. She traveled the world for a year, then returned to get her law degree from American University in Washington, DC. Lizzie is now a Humanitarian lawyer in Geneva, Switzerland. She has a lovely daughter, Zoe, and a wonderful life there. Sam and I typically see them twice a year, in Geneva and in Ouray.

Matt also graduated from CU-Boulder with a degree in journalism. He remains devoted to the Denver Broncos, and his entire family and both dogs wear blue and orange on game days. He lives in Denver now, about fifteen miles away from a kid named Peyton who ate at the tea room once. Matt and his wife Hailey have three wonderful children—Jackson, Mackenzie, and Spencer. He works in the tech sector and Hailey is a pediatric nurse. They, too, have learned to live life large.

My family never saw Ray or his father again after we pulled away from our home for the last time over three decades ago. For a long time, the Asshole in my Head pummeled my conscience as I struggled hard to forgive. I had been taught all my life to forgive and forget, that to forgive was divine. Have I finally been able to reach that noble goal after all these years? The answer is: Nope, 'fraid not. Not by most standards, anyway. It depends on one's definition of forgiveness, I suppose. If it requires feeling all warm and fuzzy about Ray and truly forgetting his terrifying acts against my family, I can say with certainty that will never happen. If it requires telling him out loud that I forgive him, well, what would be the point? I doubt he cared whether we forgave him or not. Fair enough, I guess; what Ray and his father thought of us is none of my business. I can say that none of us ever felt hatred for him, though—fear, yes; anger, most decidedly—but not hatred. Frankly, we just didn't have the energy for that.

But if forgiveness means letting go of the animosity, the bitterness, then all four of us arrived there a long time ago. I eventually concluded that it is okay not to forgive Ray. Instead, I decided never to give him permission to take up real estate in my head again. Make no mistake—this was no grandiose attempt toward altruism on my part; it was, simply put, a survival mechanism. Sometimes, forgiving someone who has wronged you is a self*ish* act; carrying that burden would have been much more detrimental to us than to anyone else. Months, sometimes years, have gone by without my even thinking of Ray or his father. Probably the thing that helped my family the most, though, was that we came out just fine on the other side. We found a lot of love waiting for us in Ouray, and that made it much easier to move past those terrible days of 1990.

I don't dream about Ray slinking around the winery at night anymore either, although I did for several years. For a while I secretly feared that he may follow us, trying to finish what he had set out to do in the Delta. But deep down, I doubted it; he wasn't one to venture out much. The horrifying dream that had kept me awake every night that summer long ago finally faded into obscurity. My recurring dream these days involves subbing in Senior English at Ouray High School and something about a novel by Marcel Proust.

One summer day in 2015, I was happy to see a letter from the Delta sitting in our mailbox. It was from Shirley's father, who had been a good friend for many years. I knew that he had recently retired as a physics professor at Delta State, and I was curious to learn how retirement suited him. In the brief note, he said, "Here is a snippet from yesterday's newspaper that you will find interesting." Glancing at the headline as I refilled my coffee cup, I wondered why he had sent it.

Who the hell was Kenneth Akridge?

CHAPTER 28

The Joy of No Joy

I sit at the computer in my sun-drenched dining room in Ouray, Colorado, looking over my work and contemplating the denouement of my story. Fourteen boxes sit on the table and lounging between two of them is our elderly cat. She watches me as I set my teacup down and gaze out the bay window. She follows my lead, purring and drinking in the warm sunshine. The light catches the little gold heart dangling from her collar, engraved with her name—Stinkerbell. She notices the brown sparrows chirping in the shrubbery outside the window. Her ears point up and her tail slowly begins to sway back and forth. I know exactly what she is thinking. So many birds . . . so little time.

The view from our dining room is stunning, providing a clear vista of Mt. Abram, peaking at nearly thirteen thousand feet. We have already had a light dusting of snow on the top. Below spreads a luxurious carpet of evergreens, with a few throw rugs of bright gold aspen thrown in for effect. I see four trucks slowly making their way down the winding switchback into town, grateful, no doubt, for having survived the infamous Red Mountain Pass just a few miles south. As I sit there quietly, I recall once asking a Ouray native if she ever grew accustomed to the postcard-worthy scenery surrounding our little town, if she ever took it for granted.

"No, Di, I don't," she responded. "I was born here eighty years ago, and I still gasp just a little when I look out my window every morning."

I hear the kitchen door open and shut, and Sam wanders in from his man cave out back, a cold one in his hand. "How's it coming?" he asks, looking over the vast disarray of papers that has been covering the large table for over a year. Not that it has bothered him in the least; Sam is easy that way.

"I think I may be about finished," I tell him.

"Really?" He looks over my shoulder at the screen, a smile on his still-handsome face. "That's great!" He kisses the top of my head and goes back to the kitchen. After 50 years of marriage, he knows when I need my space.

I examine the stack of yellowed articles I have chosen to include in my narrative. Countless others remain in the boxes, along with faded photographs that document our journey over the course of more than fourteen years. I go through them one by one, reflecting on the journalists and their kind words in recounting the life and death of The Winery Rushing and Top of the Cellar Tea Room. The latest one, the one headlining Kenneth Akridge, sits at the bottom. I pick it up and try to recall my initial thoughts when I had received it seven years earlier. I need to think about this carefully, with a clear perspective. I take a deep breath and close my eyes. How had I reacted to the news?

Shocked.

I had been deeply shocked and profoundly saddened.

Wasted lives.

Violence.

The gift that keeps on giving.

Unexpectedly, I am taken back to a time and place from long ago, my first day on an assembly line in a large, noisy factory in Ansbach, Germany. I am barely twenty years old. I have been married for one month. I have never worked at a "real" job before. I cannot understand a word of the instructions being shouted at me by a stocky, intimidating foreman in a blue jumpsuit.

I sit next to a lovely young German girl named Renata, who is watching me with sympathy as the floor supervisor stands behind me. "Macht schnell, Fräulein!" he yells. The metal press next to me is deafening. I sit on the metal stool, trying to balance little screws on their heads to send them on down the line. My hands shake as I attempt my task over and over, with no success. I finally complete the first one as the Vorarbeiter peers over my shoulder. I watch it move on to the automatic press just to my right. Just 3,199 more to go.

Schnell!

Tears slide down my face as the screws tumble once again on the next one. The assembly line continues its pace, and the metal plates stack up on my left, each hit jarring the one I am focused on. The screws topple with infuriating, persistent rhythm. Clank, clank, clank. Everyone is staring at me. I am equal parts frightened and humiliated.

Suddenly, Renata stands up, leans over, and begins setting the screws with practiced efficacy, quickly correcting my missteps. One by one, the plates move along smoothly toward the press. She smiles at me, telling me with her eyes not to pay attention to the rantings of the man standing just behind me.

"Schadenfreude," she whispers. "Macht nichts." I have no idea what she is saying, but I feel better immediately. I take a deep breath and pick up two more screws.

Schadenfreude—one of the first words I learned in German—is the word I am searching for today as I sit at the table and ponder my final words. If it has an English equivalent, I don't know what it is. In German, it is a compound noun which combines *schaden*, meaning harm or damage, with *freude*, which means joy. In short, it is the feeling of joy one derives from witnessing or learning of someone else's pain. A wicked notion perhaps, but a very real one.

I look at the newspaper clipping in my hand once again. It is about Ray's nephew, the baby boy I had worried about on Christmas Eve so long ago, born into the Russell family's house of cards just weeks following Ray's rampage. I recall that I was deeply saddened when I read the article, sent by my friend in the Delta seven years ago. It had long been my hope that Ray had done some self-reflection over the years and was living a productive life, for everyone's sake. But I was also shocked, not only by the events, but by my visceral reaction to them. As I slowly tucked the article back into the envelope, I sensed a last little sliver of fear—a minuscule fragment of dread that had remained hidden for many years—resurface, gather its belongings, and say its final goodbye.

Still, there was no schadenfreude, no cognitive dissonance, no sense of satisfaction in learning of the tragedy. Quite to the contrary. What I felt instead was a paradox of sorts, a feeling I can only describe as . . . the joy of no joy.

August 19, 2015
Bolivar Commercial
Cleveland, Mississippi
Akridge charged with murder

Kenneth Akridge II has been officially charged with three counts of murder, following the death of three family members Monday.

A spokesman for the Bolivar County Sheriff's Department said, "Shortly after 6 a.m. Monday morning, the Bolivar County Sheriff's Department received a report that a family had been murdered at 195 Sandy Road in Merigold.

"Upon arrival, deputies found three deceased victims inside the residence. The Mississippi Crime Lab was called in to process the crime scene and the Mississippi Bureau of Investigation was called to assist with the investigation."

Ackridge was detained and confessed to killing his relatives after having a domestic altercation at the home.

The victims were identified as Teresa Russell, her husband Ray Russell and Emmitt Russell, father of Ray.

AFTERWORD

Today, a sandy-haired young man sits in a cell at the infamous Parchman Prison, just a few miles down the road from where he grew up along the banks of the Sunflower River. He will likely be there for the rest of his life. Unsavory rumors abound in the Delta explaining why he murdered his grandfather, his uncle, and his uncle's wife, one hot summer night in 2015. No one but he likely knows which version, if any, holds the truth.

But just as I wondered the day I received the letter from my friend in Merigold about the murder, I still wonder: Who was Kenneth Akridge? What drove him to this violent act against his family with whom he lived at the time? Was it poverty, abuse, substance abuse? I don't know, nor am I sure that I want to, given that my family and his share such a sordid history.

What I have learned is this: Intergenerational trauma—the passing down of world views shaped by the hardships endured by one's forefathers—is real. Sometimes it is collective, sometimes it is individual; I suspect we all suffer from it to some degree. Generation after generation, we inherit in part the fears, the prejudices, and the anger of our parents, our grandparents and beyond. The child whose grandmother endured the Holocaust likely has different fears from one whose ancestors were slaves. Sometimes these fears are passed down subconsciously and sometimes they are taught. All are there to help us to cope, to survive.

Ray Russell received his inheritance, just as I received mine. Some of us, the lucky ones, were regaled with old family stories of resilience and success; their reminiscences are hopeful, amusing, intrinsically optimistic. The less fortunate were raised with family tales of hardship, hopelessness, and desperation. All these stories shape how we as individuals look at the world, how we internalize its inequities. And more importantly, these kitchen table stories impact how we respond to these inheritances.

Only Mr. Akridge knows what drove him to do what he did that August night. Perhaps not even he knows for sure. Whatever the reason, I am deeply saddened. Because deep down, I am certain that Kenneth Akridge, much more than the Rushing family, is the biggest victim of all.

And now it is he who is paying the price.

ABOUT THE AUTHOR

Photo by Sam Rushing

Diane (Di) Rushing grew up in the Mississippi Delta. After graduating from Mississippi State University in 1976, she and her husband Sam established the first winery in the state of Mississippi near Merigold, where they produced national award-winning wines for fourteen years. In 1983, Rushing opened Top of the Cellar Tea Room and published a companion cookbook featuring its recipes. In 1990, she and her young family relocated to the small mountain town of Ouray, Colorado. There, she taught high school English and psychology for twenty years and worked with her husband at Ouray Glassworks and Pottery Company. Rushing still misses Delta sunsets.